COMPREHENSION

CQ

ISSUE A: Inferring

Castles, Cabins, and Capsules

Castles, Cabins, and Capsules

THINK ABOUT: Inferring

A4

FICTION
Fall Comes to Appalachia
Her father's death brings many changes to young Mary's life—including leaving her beloved home.

A11

NONFICTION
Living and Working in Space
Have you ever wondered what it would be like to live and work in space? This article will tell you what it's like!

A18

FICTION
The Sword in the Stone
Take a step back in time with this legend about the young King Arthur.

A24

NONFICTION
Breaking New Ground: The Creative Genius of Mary Colter
Read to find out about a woman who made her mark in more ways than one!

INFERRING

Good-bye to an Old Friend

When Anna glanced at the newspaper on the kitchen table, she noticed that there was an article about one of her favorite neighborhood places, "Cozy Corner Books."

I love Cozy Corner, thought Anna. *I have to read this article.* She picked up the newspaper and began to read.

Because she is a careful reader, Anna is used to **making inferences** as she reads. As she reads the newspaper article, notice how Anna makes critical judgments and forms her own interpretation about what she is reading.

Three weeks from today, one of Mansfield's most loved buildings will become part of its history. On May 1, Cozy Corner Books, the children's bookstore that has served more than three generations of Mansfield's young in its 80-year existence, is scheduled to be torn down. Despite months of protest from many loyal Cozy Corner supporters, the new owner, Lawrence Snodgrass, has no plans to call off the demolition.

Eighty-five-year-old grandfather and life-long Mansfield resident, Charles Mennetti, remembered, "When I was a young boy, my father brought me here as a special treat, even when money was tight." As he looked fondly at the old building, Mennetti wiped a tear from behind his glasses. "I feel like I'm saying good-bye to an old friend. Mansfield sure won't be the same without it."

When asked for his own comments, Snodgrass replied, "There's nothing I can do about it. That building has to come down."

> I can't believe they're going to tear down Cozy Corner Books. It's been there ever since I was little!

> I know just how they feel. My mother took me there when I was little, too.

> What a terrible man! Doesn't he care about how much we all love Cozy Corner Books? Why does he have to tear it down?

Something has to be done, thought Anna. *Cozy Corner Books has to be saved. But what can I do?* she wondered.

Tune in later to find out what Anna does to save Cozy Corner Books. In the meantime, think about making inferences as you read the stories and articles in this issue.

Fall Comes to Appalachia:
A Story of Frontier Life

by Jean Brabham McKinney

September had come to North Carolina's Blue Ridge Mountains. The leaves were showing crimson, and the apple trees were loaded with red, gold, and yellow apples. And a change had come into the life of Mary Rogers, almost ten, and her mother, Sara—Sam Rogers, Sara's husband and Mary's father, a fine young man and a good farmer, had died suddenly of a heart attack. After a time, Sara decided to move to her mother's cabin—her childhood home— a few miles away.

"But I don't want to leave home, Ma!" cried Mary. "This is where we've always lived and where all my friends are. Why did Pa have to die and leave us?"

"That I don't know, Mary," answered Ma, wiping her eyes. "I reckon there's some things we just can't understand. Your granny will be glad to see us. She's all alone. Your Uncle Jake's goin' to bring his horse and wagon and help us move."

Mary's brown and white puppy, Honey, was lying on the floor of the cabin, close to Mary and her mother.

"I don't think Honey's goin' to like leavin' here," Mary said as she picked up the dog and hugged him.

"I hate to tell you this, Mary, but we can't take Honey with us," said Ma sadly. "Granny doesn't want any more dogs around—especially in the house. And we have to respect Granny's wishes. Miss Sally, 'round the bend, will keep him. She needs a dog and she'll be good to him. I've already talked to her."

That night, Mary cried herself to sleep with Honey snuggled in her arms.

A week later, Uncle Jake loaded Mary and Sara and their belongings in his wagon and took them across the mountains to Granny McClellan's log cabin. Granny hugged them both and cried as she embraced her daughter.

"You're too young to be a widow woman, my dear," she said.

"Granny," Mary asked, "why couldn't I bring my Honey Hound along?"

"Sugar, I've got four dogs in the yard. I don't need any more dogs around. I've cleared out a place for you and your mama's bed right close to the fireplace. And I've put two of my best patchwork quilts on top of your blankets so you'll sleep nice and warm all through the winter. It's goin' to be a cold one, that's a certainty. The bark on the north side of the trees is mighty heavy and the squirrels' tails are the bushiest I've seen in a long time."

Granny had a good rabbit-and-vegetable stew cooking in the iron pot hanging over the fire and baked apples in the Dutch oven sitting on the coals. After supper, she closed the shutters on the windows. A cold wind was howling around the house. Later, Mary snuggled in bed with her mother and cried herself to sleep.

How do you think the author wants you to feel about Mary's move? What story details does she use to make you feel this way?

"If I could just have Honey here with me," she sobbed. Granny's dogs were big and rough and not at all friendly.

"They're for Granny's protection," Ma explained. She tried to comfort Mary. "Granny's makin' you a pretty rag doll. She'll have yellow wool hair and blue button eyes."

The next day, Granny said to Ma, "There's a nice young man here in town. He's Preacher Brown's brother. Those two live together in a little cabin near the church. They both have some book learnin'. Our preacher is a sort of missionary—he travels from church to church since there's not enough preachers to go around. That's why we only have preachin' on the first Sunday of the month. I heard the preacher's brother is openin' a school real soon. He'll be teachin' in the church durin' the week for the next six weeks. Then school will be dismissed. It doesn't last very long, but maybe Mary would like to go."

"How would you like that, Mary?" Sara asked. "I want you to learn to read and write. I never had the chance to. Your pa could read a little. He would want you to read, too."

"Yes, Ma," Mary answered. "I think I'd like that."

The next Sunday, the ladies brought baskets of food with them to church. Afterward, they spread the food out on the long wooden table in the churchyard. While everybody ate, Preacher Brown introduced his brother, George, and told the congregation about the school he planned to open.

"He looks sorta like Pa," Mary whispered to her mother, who nodded in agreement.

Mary liked going to school and made friends with the other children. Sara came whenever she could and learned along with Mary.

One day George walked home with the two of them and asked Sara if she would like to go to a candy pulling at a neighbor's house the coming Friday night. Sara said yes but asked Granny if she thought it would be OK.

"Why, yes, dear," said Granny. "You can't keep mournin' forever."

On Friday night, dressed in his very best, George came for Sara in a wagon pulled by a big, black horse.

Mary thought her ma looked beautiful in the new dress, bonnet, and coat Granny had made for her.

The cabin where the candy pulling was being held was lit by a roaring fire in the big fireplace. The house was already filled with couples gathered around a long table where thick molasses stood in a large container. Following the lead of the other couples, George and Sara greased their hands in lard, and George made a ball out of the molasses. Each held one end of the ball and pulled out long ribbons of candy, then spread them out on a large greased plate and waited for the candy to harden into yellow sticks of rock candy.

"We'll take some home to Mary and Granny," said George.

After the refreshments, the fiddlers started playing and the square dancing began. It lasted until almost midnight.

Fall gradually passed and winter blew in. The blue mountains were covered with white snow. Granny worked at her loom, weaving wool thread into cloth. And George kept coming to see Sara. Then one night, Sara told Mary and Granny that she and George were going to get married.

"And you'll have a pa again," Ma said to Mary. "It'll be awhile before George and I get married," Ma said. "We're goin' to have to get a cabin built first."

The community soon got the news of the upcoming wedding by way of the grapevine, and a house-raising was planned. In the spring, every strong, able man in the area volunteered, and in two days, the cabin was built.

> Can you predict what might happen next? What clues does the author give to help you make that prediction?

On the first day, the men had gone out into the woods and cut down the trees. First, they cut the logs to size and notched the corners to keep them from rolling away. Then they carried the logs to the site of the cabin and put up the framing.

On the second day, the men finished the house and roof and built a big stone chimney out of rocks and red mud. Finally, they added a small front porch.

The next day, the preacher married his brother, George, to Sara. It was a special day for the whole community. And that evening, the newlyweds had a big housewarming with fiddling and square dancing for the folks who had helped with the house-raising.

Two days later, Sara and George came over in their horse-drawn wagon. Granny had packed Mary's clothes and everything was ready to go.

Mary kissed Granny goodbye. "Come back to see me real soon," Granny said. "I'll miss you, my precious child."

"I'll miss you too, Granny," Mary whispered, close to tears.

Then George lifted Mary up to the driver's seat between him and Sara. Sitting close to Ma, Mary felt better.

They rode for a little while, made a sharp turn, then George said, "Here's our new home, Mary."

She could hardly believe her eyes. Before her, surrounded by pines and hickory trees, was a pretty log cabin with a cloud of gray smoke curling out of its chimney.

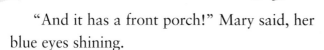

"And it has a front porch!" Mary said, her blue eyes shining.

"We'll enjoy sittin' on it next summer," said Sara.

"You two go on in and get warm," George said, "and I'll bring in your things, Mary."

As Mary hopped up on the front porch, she thought she heard a dog bark.

Oh, if only that was Honey's bark! Mary thought, her heart still aching for him.

Ma opened the door, and Mary saw the inside of their new cabin—a fire was burning in the fireplace, and the whole room was filled with the smell of stew and applesauce cooking in the iron pots hanging over the fire.

When George came in, he put Mary's belongings down on her big rope bed with its fresh straw mattress and its blankets and quilts.

"I have one more thing to bring in," said George. "I'll be right back."

"This is your side of the room," Ma said, "right close to the fireplace."

Ma helped Mary take off her coat and bonnet and hung them on the hooks on the wall near her bed.

What do you think George will bring in? What makes you think so?

"And how do you like our wood floor?" Ma asked. "It's much nicer than the dirt ones we've had."

"Oh, yes," said Mary, "it's nice and clean and warm." Then she stopped to listen. "Ma, I hear a dog barkin'."

Suddenly, George opened the door. Wiggling in his arms was Honey Hound!

"George went all the way back to Miss Sally's house to get him for you," said Ma. "George really wants you to be happy, Sugar."

Honey gave an excited bark and jumped into Mary's arms and licked her face.

That night, snuggled in bed with Honey beside her, Mary sighed. She was truly happy to be in her new house with her new pa, her ma, and her Honey Hound! ◉

Was your prediction correct? If not, reread the first part of the page to find any clues you may have missed.

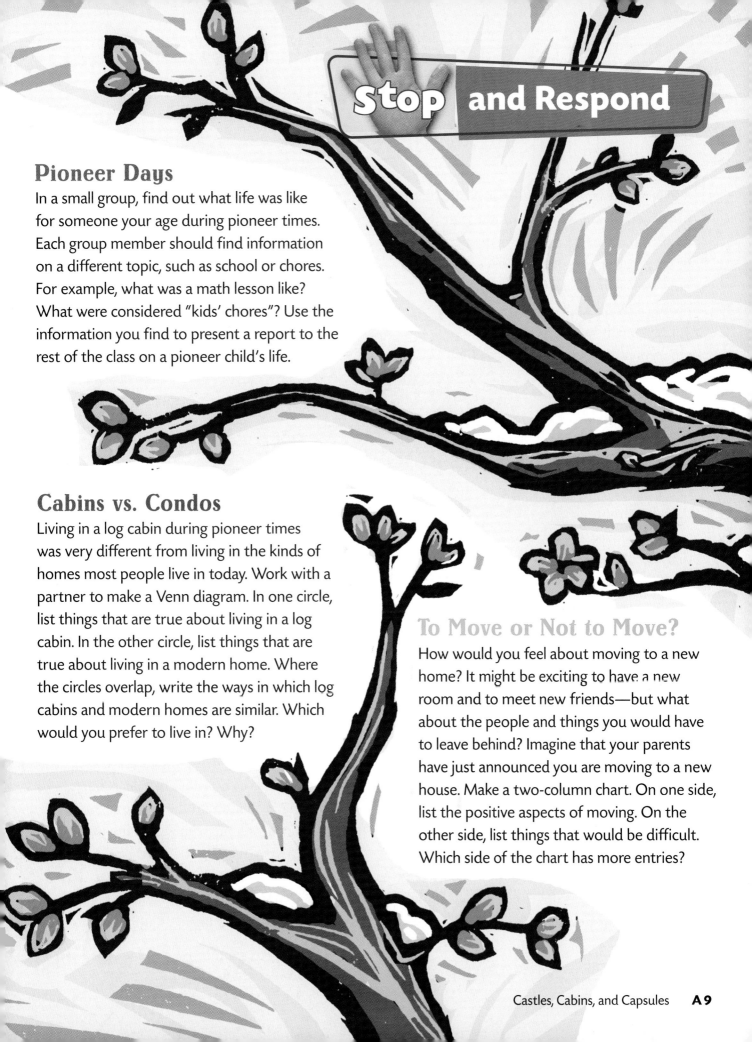

Pioneer Days

In a small group, find out what life was like for someone your age during pioneer times. Each group member should find information on a different topic, such as school or chores. For example, what was a math lesson like? What were considered "kids' chores"? Use the information you find to present a report to the rest of the class on a pioneer child's life.

Cabins vs. Condos

Living in a log cabin during pioneer times was very different from living in the kinds of homes most people live in today. Work with a partner to make a Venn diagram. In one circle, list things that are true about living in a log cabin. In the other circle, list things that are true about living in a modern home. Where the circles overlap, write the ways in which log cabins and modern homes are similar. Which would you prefer to live in? Why?

To Move or Not to Move?

How would you feel about moving to a new home? It might be exciting to have a new room and to meet new friends—but what about the people and things you would have to leave behind? Imagine that your parents have just announced you are moving to a new house. Make a two-column chart. On one side, list the positive aspects of moving. On the other side, list things that would be difficult. Which side of the chart has more entries?

Little Cabins, Big Impact

During America's pioneer days, the promise of adventure and fortune led thousands of settlers to move west. Many settlers came to believe that opportunity lay just over the next hill—or the hill after that. This belief kept people moving west for many years.

As quickly as pioneers settled an area, some moved on to another. This constant movement west could never have happened so quickly without a type of house that the pioneers could build quickly, using only the materials they found nearby.

The pioneer's choice of shelter—the log cabin—has since become a symbol of America's frontier heritage. It has also come to stand for the ideals of practicality, self-reliance, and independence—ideals that many believe are uniquely American.

For the American pioneers who had plenty of timber, a house built entirely of wood was the most practical choice. But pioneer homes also had to stand up to harsh winters. Log cabins were made by laying logs in horizontal layers with their corners notched and fitted together. Cracks were sealed with moss, mud, or other materials, so log cabins were as airtight and winter-proof as a house could be in pioneer times.

Because pioneers moved often, they needed to build their homes quickly. One person could chop down the trees and prepare the cellar and foundation, but raising the heavy logs for the sides of the cabin required some neighborly help. Cabin-raisings became a special social event that created a sense of community among the pioneers. While the men assembled the cabin walls, the women cooked, and the children fetched small tools. Cabin-raisings were true examples of communities working together.

Life in a log cabin was hard for frontier families, but it was also good. Families were close-knit, and everyone shared in life's joys, such as weddings, births, and celebrations. Because there was no radio or television, families had to entertain themselves. This meant playing simple games, playing musical instruments, or reading together. And though there were difficult times, such as illness and death, pioneers could always count on the help of caring neighbors.

Participants at the United States Space Camp operate controls in a space shuttle cockpit on a simulated mission.

Living and Working in Space

by Karen Hoenecke

For centuries, people have gazed at the stars and dreamed of traveling to distant planets. Today, those dreams have become a reality through the commitment and hard work of many dedicated scientists. In just a few short decades, humans have made great advances toward living and working in outer space.

In the late 1950s, the United States and the Soviet Union began to compete for superiority in space. Although this "space race" between American astronauts and Soviet cosmonauts lasted only until the late 1970s, the two countries compiled an impressive list of outer space achievements: orbiting Earth, walking in space, landing on the Moon, walking on the Moon, and living in space for many weeks at a time.

Still, living conditions in space present many challenges. Near-weightlessness, also known as "zero gravity," is one of the greatest challenges. On Earth, for example, if you lifted your bicycle off the ground, you would notice the pull of gravity. Your bike would feel heavy. Eventually you would have to set it down, and it would stay where you put it. But in space, there is no gravity, so things seem weightless. You would be able to lift your bicycle with ease, but you probably wouldn't find it where you left it. Your bike would probably be floating around the spacecraft—and might even hit you in the head!

Left: Astronaut Jeffrey S. Ashby takes a moment for a snack while on his way to the International Space Station.

Top: Astronaut Yuri P. Gidzenko works with computers on the International Space Station.

Middle: This camper at the United States Space Camp is riding in a chair astronauts use when fixing satellites.

The near-weightlessness of outer space has forced scientists to look for ways to make living and working in space easier. For example, inside the spacecraft, guide lines are often strung across the cabin so that astronauts can hold on and pull themselves across the room. To make standing on the floor of the cabin easier, a sticky material can be attached to the astronauts' shoes and also to the floor. To ensure the safety of the crew, tools and equipment are strapped to a wall to prevent them from floating around the spacecraft.

Zero gravity might sound like fun, but it does take some getting used to. One way to experience the sensation of near-weightlessness is to try moving underwater. Although your initial attempts might feel clumsy, gradually you would learn to move around more easily. Another way for astronauts to experience weightlessness is during a steep dive in a jet. When the jet heads downward at a high rate of speed, its passengers experience the weightlessness of space. This gives astronauts an opportunity to practice moving around, eating, and drinking in a weightless environment.

Despite these exercises, many astronauts still experience *space adaptation syndrome,* or space sickness. Fortunately, space sickness lasts for only a few days, and scientists have found that motion sickness medicine often helps relieve this problem.

How knowledgeable does the author seem to be about life in space? How can you be sure the information in the article is accurate and up to date?

From left to right: James Voss, Yuri Usachev, and Susan Helms boarded the International Space Station in March 2001.

Eating and drinking in space pose some interesting problems, too. Imagine snacking on peanuts and lemonade when suddenly a peanut slips out of your hand. Do you chase after the floating peanut first, or do you close off the clamp on the end of your straw to stop the lemonade from coming up and out of the straw?

In the early days of space exploration, food was often freeze-dried or stuffed into tubes to prevent these types of mishaps. Today, thanks to improvements in packaging that allow food to stay fresh longer and to be eaten before it floats away, space food is very much like what we eat on Earth. Single-serving containers keep astronauts' foods fresh and make them easy to eat. Several dishes are included on a tray that the astronaut attaches to his or her leg. Astronaut silverware is like ours, only it includes scissors for opening packages.

Still, long trips into space can often have negative effects on astronauts, both physically and mentally. In outer space, the bones and muscles of the human body can weaken. Strenuous daily exercises and a special diet can help eliminate or reduce some of these problems. Social contact with loved ones back on Earth has also proven beneficial in helping astronauts maintain healthy mental attitudes.

When space exploration began, only a few expert pilots with many hours of flying experience were chosen to become astronauts. Today, people from a variety of other occupations are needed for work in space. Just as hospitals require doctors, nurses, secretaries, custodians, and others to run smoothly, future space explorations will require many different kinds of workers as well.

Space employees of the future might be needed to navigate the spacecraft or perform scientific experiments in space. Scientists are needed to study the universe from the atmosphere-free conditions in space, to determine how our universe was formed and whether life exists beyond our Earth. Others will be required to activate equipment in space, dock space

Space travel has taken us to the Moon—and beyond.

vehicles, transport supplies, and maintain and repair equipment. Future space expeditions will also require individuals who can refuel and launch visiting spacecraft, while others may be expected to work outside the unit. Someday, there may even be a need for farmers to tend livestock and harvest crops in space!

The first crew moved into the International Space Station near the end of 2000. Built through the cooperative efforts of the United States, Russia, Canada, Japan, and several European countries, this large space station provides opportunities for astronauts from many countries to work and learn together. Maybe you could even envision a career for yourself at this space station, working with other astronauts in a spirit of international unity.

What is the author's attitude toward life in space? What information in the text leads you to believe this?

People used to say, "The sky's the limit." In space exploration, however, the sky may *not* be the limit. Some scientists believe that future space endeavors might include building large space colonies, a Moon research base, manned spaceships to Mars and its moons, and a system of interplanetary travel.

Do the adventures and challenges of living and working in space excite you? Would you like to curl up and sleep in a bed that has to be attached to the wall? Would you like to hear daily wake-up songs piped into your spacecraft each day from Mission Control back on Earth? Then you might want to pursue a career in space. But you don't have to wait for adulthood to investigate further. You can read more on the NASA Web site to learn about careers that are "out of this world!" ○

What do you think the author's purpose was in writing this article? After reading it, how do you feel about living and working in space?

Space Fitness

One problem that astronauts face after a long time in space is the weakening of their muscles. This happens because astronauts do not use their muscles to support their bodies as they work and perform other activities in space. Design a new exercise that astronauts could do in space. Make sure that your exercise helps strengthen muscles without the help of gravity. Then have the class try several of the exercises to decide which one would be most effective in space.

A Space-y Job

Working in space requires certain qualities in a person. Write a "Help Wanted" ad for one of the jobs that might be available in space in the future. Look at the classified ads in your local newspaper to help you. Be sure to include a list of job requirements.

Hazards of the Job

What would be the scariest part of living in space? Would it be zero gravity? Would it be knowing you were millions of miles away from home? Or would it be learning that there really *are* aliens in space? With a few classmates, write a short play that dramatizes your group's ideas. Then act out your play for the class.

blast off!

Earth is becoming a very crowded place—too many people and not enough space. Or is there enough *space*? If we look to outer space to solve our *space* problem, we might be able to ease the overcrowding. So here's your challenge—design a space settlement community that will be ready for habitation in the year 2030 on the Moon.

WHAT YOU WILL NEED:

★ a group of classmates to work with
★ poster or illustration board
★ markers, colored pencils, crayons, paints
★ notebook and pens or pencils
★ a fantastic imagination!

WHAT YOU NEED TO THINK ABOUT:

★ kinds of buildings to include (homes, schools, stores, hospitals, theaters, sports arenas, etc.)
★ how food will be produced
★ how water will be supplied
★ how energy will be generated
★ forms of transportation
★ a great name for your settlement, or colony
★ anything else your fantastic imagination comes up with!

Now you're ready to blast off to the future—who knows, maybe *you* will be one of the first space colonists! You just might be the first teacher, carpenter, farmer, or veterinarian to settle on the Moon!

INFERRING

The Other Side of the Story

After reading the article about Cozy Corner Books being torn down, Anna decided to write a letter to the editor. But when she picked up that morning's paper, she saw the following letter on the editorial page. Read the inferences Anna made as she read it.

To the wonderful people of Mansfield,

My great-grandfather, George Booker, opened Cozy Corner Books over 80 years ago. Over the years, my entire family has been involved in some way with Cozy Corner, and we have all been delighted to provide an inviting place for the people of Mansfield to share a love of books.

Unfortunately, my wife and I have reached an age when many of our friends have long since retired. Since we have no children of our own, we have had to face the fact that it is time to let Cozy Corner go. Such an old building has been harder to maintain as the years have gone by, and we no longer have the time, money, or energy to keep Cozy Corner.

Fortunately, the new owner, Mr. Lawrence Snodgrass, has many exciting plans for a wonderful new bookstore that will stand in the place of the old Cozy Corner building. The new bookstore, Cozy Commons, will have books for all ages, the latest technology, and an auditorium for poetry and book readings.

So it is not the end, but a new beginning for an old and dear friend. We hope you will join us in welcoming Mr. Snodgrass, and that you will come to love Cozy Commons as much as you loved Cozy Corner.

A fond farewell,
Alfred P. Booker

Oh, this is a letter from Mr. Booker, the owner of Cozy Corner. I'll bet he's upset that the new owner is tearing his building down.

Wait a minute. Mr. Booker doesn't seem upset at all. In fact, he sounds kind of relieved. I guess it's kind of selfish to want the Bookers to keep Cozy Corner just because we love it so much.

I didn't realize that the new owner was building a new bookstore. The new building sounds awesome. I might like going there, too.

Maybe Mr. Snodgrass is not such a bad person after all. I'm glad there will still be a great book store here!

Think about the many kinds of inferences you make as you read. You may use words on the page as a starting point. But, like Anna, try to go beyond the words on the page to **make inferences** about the people, places, and events you read about. By combining the text with your own background knowledge and experience, you can make your own judgments about the deeper meaning of the text.

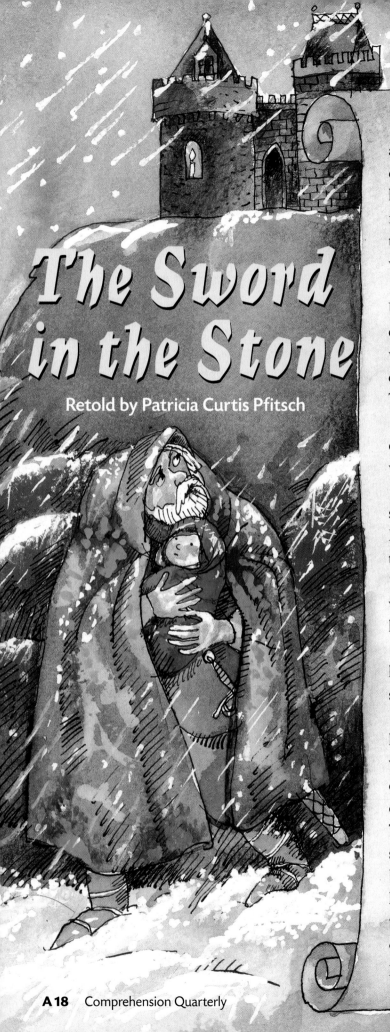

The Sword in the Stone

Retold by Patricia Curtis Pfitsch

The wind was fierce, and the icy snow stung as it pelted the old man's face. He pulled his dark green cloak closer to block the cold. Before him rose the forbidding stone walls of the castle, fortress of the high king of Britain. Behind him, the cliff dropped hundreds of feet to the crashing waves of the Irish Sea.

The old man looked up. He could see King Uther's soldiers on the battlements. He moved closer to the walls. If he were seen, his mission would fail. In the nearest tower, the light of a candle flickered in a narrow, arched window. That was the signal—it was time.

The old man pounded on a small wooden door that was hidden in a corner of the castle walls. It opened, and he slipped inside.

A woman came down the narrow stone stairway cradling a small bundle in her arms. Her eyes glistened with tears in the smoky torchlight. She handed the bundle to the old man. "The queen fears for his life, Lord Merlin," she whispered. "He needs your protection from the king's enemies."

The woman uncovered the baby's face and kissed his cheek. "He's a fine, strong lad," she said, touching his dark hair.

"All will be well," Merlin said. "I will keep him safely hidden." He covered the child's face with the blanket. A young page jumped to open the thick wooden door, and Merlin went out into the midwinter storm. The heavy iron latch clanged shut. Merlin hugged his tiny bundle close, wrapped his green cloak around them both, and headed down the narrow winding path away from the castle.

> How did you feel about Merlin after reading this part of the story? Why might the author want you to feel this way?

Twelve-year-old Arthur was the first to hear the clatter of hooves as two knights on horseback approached Sir Ector's castle. He leaped up, let his book slide to the floor, and ran to the library window.

"Lower the drawbridge!" one of the knights yelled. "We have messages for you!"

Arthur's dark hair flopped into his eyes as he strained to see through the thin opening in the thick stone walls. Windows were narrow to keep out arrows if the castle came under attack, but they were useless if you wanted a good view of the courtyard. Arthur raced to the small door leading out onto the battlements.

He ran along the narrow walkway between the thick castle walls and the half-walls that protected the soldiers on watch. Here he could see everything in the courtyard below. He listened eagerly. Sir Ector, his guardian, kept a close watch on him, rarely allowing him outside the castle walls. Maybe now he would find out what was happening in the world!

"What is your message?" Sir Ector asked.

"In the years since the high king's death," the knight announced, "all of Britain has been in chaos."

"Everyone knows that," Arthur grumbled. The knights had been fighting with each other ever since King Uther died. Outlaws ran free in the countryside, and there was talk of war. Everyone hoped that Lord Merlin, the king's advisor, would bring forth Uther's only son and heir, but nobody could find either Merlin or the boy. People thought Merlin had magically spirited the child away.

"The Archbishop of Canterbury has proclaimed a tournament on the occasion of the midwinter holiday," the knight shouted, reading

from a parchment marked with a heavy gold seal. "Let us use our weapons in sport, not in anger!"

"We will come," said Ector. He waved his hand to dismiss the knights. They turned their horses, clattered across the drawbridge, and were gone.

A tournament! Arthur's eyes gleamed. Knights would compete on foot and on horseback to see who was the strongest. Everyone in Britain would be there. He ran to the corner tower and down the narrow, winding stairs that led to the Great Hall where the household gathered to eat.

He burst into the room, but it was empty. "They must be in the solarium!" he panted. He raced to the sunny room at the far end of the Great Hall and found Sir Ector talking with his son, Kay.

"You'll do well," Sir Ector was saying. "You have a strong sword arm."

"Can I go, too?" Arthur said, straightening his tunic and pushing his hair out of his eyes. "I won't be any trouble," he begged. "I promise."

Sir Ector was silent. He stroked his beard. "You'll be thirteen at midwinter," he said, almost to himself. "Maybe it's time." He turned to the boy and said, "Yes, Arthur. You may go as Kay's squire."

Arthur bowed to Kay. "I'm at your service, my lord," he said, grinning. He was going to the tournament!

Kay grunted. "We'll see if you can obey," he said, but he gave Arthur a playful slap on the arm. "Let's go take a look at my armor."

Preparations for the contest took months, but finally Arthur was riding with Sir Ector and Kay onto the enormous tournament grounds in London.

What kind of person do you think Arthur is? What information in the text did you use to decide this?

Everywhere he looked, he saw brightly colored banners and knights on horseback. Arthur proudly carried Kay's standard—the green and yellow flag fluttered in the wind. It was warm for midwinter, and the sun shone in a clear blue sky.

Suddenly, Kay jerked his horse to a standstill. He turned to Arthur, and his face was white. "I've forgotten my sword," he whispered. "In all the excitement, I must have left it at the inn."

"Your sword?" Arthur gave him a horrified look. Without his sword, Kay could not compete in the contests. "How could you . . . ?"

"Just go back and get it," interrupted Kay.

"I will," Arthur said. He handed Kay the flag, touched his pony's sides with his heels, and galloped out of the grounds.

But when he got to the inn, he found everything closed up. "Now what will I do?" Arthur wailed. "Kay must have a sword!"

He started back, looking around the town. Surely he could find a sword somewhere! He had almost passed the old cathedral when he glanced inside the yard. What was that?

He dismounted and opened the big iron gate. For a moment he thought he saw an old man in a green cloak in the doorway of the church, but when he looked again, the man was gone. The churchyard was empty, except for an old, moss-covered stone. And sticking out of the stone was a sword!

There were words carved into the stone, but Arthur didn't stop to read them. He grabbed the handle of the sword and pulled. To his surprise, it slid easily out of the stone. He hopped on his pony, and with the sword in one hand and his pony's reins in the other, he thundered back to the tournament grounds.

What do you think will happen when Arthur brings back the sword he pulled from the stone?

Kay was waiting at the entrance. "Good," he said, reaching out for the sword.

Arthur handed it to him, expecting Kay to smile. But as Kay examined the blade, his face turned whiter than before. Without a word, Kay rode over to Sir Ector.

"Father," he said, his voice husky. "This is the sword from the stone."

Sir Ector stared, first at Kay and then at the sword. "Where did you get that?" he whispered.

Arthur heard the tension in his voice, and bit his lip. The sword must be valuable, Arthur thought. Did they think he'd stolen it?

Kay looked at the sword, then at Arthur. "I forgot my sword," he admitted, "and I sent Arthur back for it. He brought me this."

"I'm sorry sir," Arthur said. "I'll take it right back!"

At that moment, Sir Ector was bumped from behind by another knight. He lifted the sword. "Watch out, Lot," Sir Ector growled.

Sir Lot's eyes widened. "The sword in the stone!" His voice rose. "How did you get it?"

Suddenly, all the knights in the enclosure were shouting at Sir Ector, Kay, and Arthur. From the deafening roar, it was clear that everyone but Arthur recognized the sword. Arthur wished he'd never seen it. Sir Ector would probably send him home before the tournament even began!

"Come with us," Sir Ector shouted. The crowd followed them to the churchyard.

In silence the knights marched through the gate. Arthur glanced up to see the old man in the green cloak peering from one of the church windows. "Put the sword back," Sir Ector croaked. Arthur's hand shook, but he took the sword. With one thrust, he shoved it back into the stone.

Sir Ector swallowed. He turned to Kay. "Now you try to pull it out."

Kay grabbed the handle and pulled. His face turned red as he struggled, but the sword did not move an inch. Then Sir Ector tried.

WHOEVER PULLS THIS SWORD FROM THIS STONE IS THE RIGHTFUL KING OF ALL BRITAIN

Other knights stepped up, but not one could free the sword.

Sir Ector nodded at Arthur. Arthur stepped up, gripped the sword, and . . . it slid easily from the stone. He held it up, and the blade glinted in the weak winter sun. He heard everyone in the crowd gasp, then sigh. He turned and found that all the knights, even Sir Ector and Kay, were on their knees, bowing to him.

"What . . . what are you doing?" Arthur's voice trembled.

Sir Ector said, "This sword appeared in the churchyard when King Uther died. Read the words that are carved there."

Arthur brushed away the moss. *"Whoever pulls this sword from this stone,"* he read in a small voice, *"is the rightful king of all Britain."* He looked at his guardian. "I don't understand."

Why do you think all the knights have bowed to Arthur? What do you think is special about the sword?

A cold wind made Arthur shiver, and suddenly the old man in the green cloak stood before him. "My name is Merlin," he said. "You are the son of King Uther and Queen Igraine," he said. "I brought you to Sir Ector soon after your birth. I knew your father was going to die, and I had to hide you until you were old enough to take the throne."

Arthur stared at the old man. "I am the high king of Britain? Me?" His voice was almost a squeak.

Sir Ector touched Arthur's shoulder. "Merlin never told me who you were," he said, "but I had my suspicions." He turned to the knights. "I have known this boy since his birth. He will make a fine king."

The knights rose to their feet, and their shout was a mighty roar. "Hail to King Arthur!"

And so it was that the boy Arthur became the high king of all Britain.

What kind of king do you think Arthur will be? What evidence in the text did you use to decide this?

Dictionary of Castle Terms

What exactly is a solarium? How does a drawbridge work? Reread the story "The Sword in the Stone," looking for words related to castles. Then use a variety of sources, including books, encyclopedias, and the Internet to create a dictionary of castle terms. Include an illustration for each of your words.

A Castle in the Air

Use the story details from "The Sword in the Stone" to draw a picture of the fortress of the high king of Britain. Be sure to include the solarium, the steep cliffs behind the castle, the drawbridge, and the huge gate.

Will the Real King Arthur Please Stand Up?

With a group of friends, act out the scene in which Arthur discovers that he is king of all Britain. Include the parts of Sir Ector, Kay, the other knights, Merlin, and of course, Arthur. Take turns with group members role-playing the different characters. Which classmate is the most believable king?

Breaking New Ground:

The Creative Genius of

Mary Colter

by Katacha Díaz

The construction of the steel framework for the Watchtower **Inset:** Mary Colter, artisan

The Grand Canyon in Arizona, one of Earth's seven wonders, attracts millions of visitors each year from around the world. Tourists are dazzled by the beauty of the colorful buttes and mesas, so it takes something very special to make them look away from these spectacular natural wonders. Yet, rising on the edge of a nearby cliff, there is a stone tower that looks as ancient and as beautiful as the canyon itself.

This 70-foot, steel-framed building known as "the Watchtower" stands at the edge of the canyon with unparalleled 360-degree views. It holds a gift shop where tourists stop to purchase souvenirs of their

Grand Canyon adventure. Yet few people realize that this ancient-looking building with Native American carvings on the exterior was built in the twentieth century. The Watchtower is the creation of multitalented architect and designer Mary Colter.

Mary Elizabeth Jane Colter was born in Pittsburgh, Pennsylvania, in 1869. Her parents, William and Rebecca Colter, had emigrated to the U.S. from Ireland and eventually settled in St. Paul, Minnesota.

It was in St. Paul that Mary became fascinated with Native American culture and art. After a family friend gave her several dozen Sioux drawings, the artwork became Mary's prized possessions. When a smallpox epidemic broke out in the Sioux community, Mary's mother burned all of the family's Native American gifts to prevent the spread of the dreaded disease. Mary, however, couldn't bear to part with her drawings, so she hid them under the mattress of her bed. It was not until many years later that her mother learned that Mary had saved the Sioux drawings. Mary Colter cherished these drawings throughout her life, and today they are part of an art collection at Eastern Montana College.

Mary's father worked as a city sewer inspector in St. Paul, and the family lived modestly. But in 1886, when Mary was seventeen years old, her father died unexpectedly.

Mary's mother worked as a hat maker, and her older sister, Harriet, worked as a seamstress. But without William's salary, it was difficult for the three women to make ends meet.

How can the author know this information about Mary Colter's life? Who do you think originally provided this information about Mary Colter?

Above: The Watchtower was completed in 1932.
Inset: Mary Colter's sketch of mural figures were later painted in the Watchtower.

The fireplace Mary Colter designed for Bright Angel Lodge in 1935

Mary was passionate about art, and it was one of her favorite subjects in school. Mary's teachers had encouraged her to pursue a career in art, and she wanted to attend the California School of Design in San Francisco. The school offered a four-year program in art and design with a teaching degree upon graduation. And it was also one of the few art schools in those days that accepted female students. Mary Colter was only fourteen years old when she graduated from high school, and her parents felt that she was too young to go away to school. After her father died, however, Mary convinced her mother and Harriet to send her to art school. She was confident that when she graduated, she would be able to get a job teaching art and design to help support her family.

So Mary went to San Francisco to attend the California School of Design. After she graduated, she took a teaching position in Wisconsin. Mary also loved to travel, and one year she returned to San Francisco to visit a friend. While she was there, Mary received a commission to design a display for a collection of Native American baskets. An executive from the Fred Harvey Company saw the display and liked it very much. He wrote to Mary to see if she would like to work on the company's new project. The Harvey Company, he wrote, needed an interior decorator. They were looking for someone who was creative and knowledgeable about Native American arts and crafts. Mary Colter, they believed, was the right person for the job.

So Mary was hired as the interior decorator for the Alvarado Hotel's new building in Albuquerque, New Mexico. Her job was to design creative ways to display the Harvey Company's Native American artifact collection. Mary's imagination and attention to detail helped her design beautiful displays, and her first assignment was a huge success.

How do you feel so far about Mary Colter? What story details do you think influenced you most?

Three years later, Mary was invited to design the Native American gift shop at the Grand Canyon. For this project, Mary wanted to create an actual replica of a Hopi dwelling so that tourists would have a glimpse of the "real" Southwest. With the help of Hopi workers, Hopi House was built with natural materials that blend into their surroundings. It has ladders that lead from one tiered roof to another and floors that look like mud but are actually made out of cement. And from the inside, the roof looks like it has been built from twigs and logs! To make sure she got all the details right, Mary consulted with a Hopi scholar. Today, Hopi House is used to exhibit a collection of Native American art.

In 1910, at the age of 41, Mary was offered a full-time job with the Fred Harvey Company. This was a dream come true for Mary who, as the company's chief architect and interior designer, worked on hotels, gift shops, dining rooms, and rest stops along the route of the new Santa Fe Railway.

Mary rode on horseback to investigate potential building sites and spent time sketching the landscape and gathering information for her designs. During these trips, Mary wore riding pants, a long jacket, and boots—clothing that was very unusual for women of that time. She also wore a big Stetson cowboy hat pulled down over her ears. Mary loved to wear Native American jewelry, and over the years, had many

Above: Interior views of Hopi House
Below: Hopi House, designed by Mary Colter in 1905, was built with natural materials that blend into their surroundings.

Castles, Cabins, and Capsules

beautiful rings, bracelets, and necklaces specially made for her. Before her death, Mary donated her jewelry collection to the Mesa Verde Museum in Colorado.

Mary Colter paid close attention to every detail in her projects. If she saw a stone that didn't look right during the construction of a building, she would ask the workers to remove it and replace it with one she thought looked better. Some of the people who worked for Mary found her to be stubborn and somewhat demanding, but in the end, they all had great respect and admiration for her work.

How do you think the author feels about Mary Colter? Do you think the author tried to influence you to feel this way?

Mary's creative genius became even more evident when she submitted plans for a new Grand Canyon building. Mary decided to place the limestone building on the edge of the canyon so that it would appear to be part of the natural landscape. Built on several levels, the building called the Watchtower has a low roof where cactus and sage plants grow and is surrounded by terraces. Visitors are able to stroll in and out of the building while they admire the spectacular and colorful scenery of the Grand Canyon.

Mary Colter never married. After 40 years of working for the Fred Harvey Company, she retired to Santa Fe, New Mexico, where she died at the age of eighty-nine. Mary Colter had spent her life pursuing her passion for architecture and interior design, and she broke new ground in a field that was then dominated by men. Today, 11 of her buildings are included in the National Register of Historic Places, and her genius lives on in the legacy she has left across the American Southwest. ○

Above: Phantom Ranch, designed by Mary Colter in 1922. Inset: Mary Colter at age 50 **Facing page:** Lookout Studio, constructed in 1914, on the edge of the Grand Canyon.

Stop and Respond

Mary Colter Gallery

Find an architectural history book and do some research about the structures that Mary Colter designed. If possible, make color copies of the photographs and use them to create a gallery of her work. Write a caption for each photo that lists the structure's name, the date it was completed, and the things that make it unique.

Design It!

Imagine that you are an illustrator hired to design a jacket for a book about Mary Colter. Use your artistic skills to illustrate a book cover that shows the kind of person that Mary Colter was. Think about her personality and her accomplishments. Your book jacket design should catch a reader's attention and make him or her want to read more about this amazing woman.

Lessons Learned

Mary Colter followed her dream and eventually became famous for her work. She was determined to be successful in a profession that was difficult for women to enter. What lessons can you learn from her story? Write a paragraph about it in your journal.

Let's Write

Capsule of History

Imagine that your class is putting together a time capsule to be opened in 2050. Write something to the people in the future that will give them clues about today's world. You could write a description of what life is like for fifth graders today or make a list of five things you could not live without. Or how about predictions about what life might be like in the year 2050? Use your imagination and writing skills to help preserve history for future generations.

The Adventures of Luna Spacewalker

The cartoon character Luna Spacewalker has been informed by Galaxy Control that her next mission is to help create a system of interplanetary travel. Work with a partner to write and illustrate a comic strip that describes how Luna does this. Remember to use speech balloons for dialogue.

Home Away From Home

If you could live in any kind of dwelling you choose for one month, what would you choose? Would it be a Sioux tepee on the plains of Nebraska? or a dark, mysterious castle in Ireland? or a safari lodge in Africa? Gather details about the unique dwelling you choose. Then write a letter to a friend or relative to persuade them to join you on your great adventure!

Making Connections

More Books

Chambers, Catherine E. *Log Cabin Home: Pioneers in the Wilderness.* Troll, 1998.

Glenn, Patricia Brown. *Under Every Roof: A Kid's Style and Field Guide to the Architecture of American Houses.* Preservation Press, 1993.

Green, Roger Lancelyn. *King Arthur and His Knights of the Round Table.* Puffin, 1995.

Lorenz, Albert. *House: Showing How People Have Lived Throughout History with Examples Drawn from the Lives of Legendary Men and Women.* Harry N. Abrams, 1998.

On the Web

NASA Space Camp
http://www.NASA.gov
http://www.spacecamp.com

Medieval Castles
http://www.medievalcastles.net

Women in Architecture
http://www.womenswire.com/watch/lin.html

Across the Curriculum

History
With your friends, organize a history-mystery tour of your community. Identify five historical buildings that are fairly well known in your town. Create clues that highlight a particular feature of each building, such as a turret, an unusual roof, or a colorful door. Challenge your classmates to identify each building, either by reading the clues or by visiting the buildings.

Health
What if you and a friend went on a shuttle mission into space? What would you eat? Do you think astronauts still eat freeze-dried meals from tiny tubes? Guess again! Find out for yourself what foods astronauts can choose from by visiting http://library.thinkquest.org/50001/FoodFact.htm on the Web. Then use the list of foods and the Food Guide Pyramid to plan a day of healthful meals for you and your friend.

Castles in the Sand

You might never see an ancient castle like the one in "The Sword in the Stone," but you can build a pretty amazing sand castle that will impress your friends!

Here's how!

You will need:

- a big section of a beach or a large sandbox
- a pail
- fine, silty sand
- a garden trowel
- carving tools, such as old kitchen utensils and paint scrapers
- smoothing tools, such as old paint brushes

How to do it:

1.
If you're building your castle on the beach, dig down to the place where water starts seeping into the hole from the bottom. If you're using a sandbox, mix sand and water together in a bucket. In either place, use both hands to scoop a huge handful of very wet sand toward you. Use this sand to start building a mound.

2.
Flatten handfuls of wet sand into pancakes by jiggling them gently. This gets the water to spread out evenly over the sand pancake. To make a tower, stack these pancakes together and smooth over the place where you put them together. Use smaller handfuls near the top to make the tower narrow.

3.
To make the walls, pull out more wet handfuls of sand from the hole or the bucket. Hold the sand between your hands and jiggle it into a brick shape. Lay the bricks end to end, and then on top of each row, until the wall is tall enough. To make stairs, carve a ramp into one of the walls and then cut the ramp into steps.

4.
To make a turret, form a cone at the top of a tower so it looks like a very pointy roof. Do the same thing on the opposite side of the tower.

5.
Decorate your castle by carving details into the sand wherever you want them. Use your carving tools to add windows and doors, and if you want, add objects from the beach, like shells, driftwood, and sea glass, to your castle.

Go Away!

THINK ABOUT: Synthesizing

B4

FICTION

Andy Wampler, Daydreamer

Do you ever find yourself daydreaming? Read what happens when Andy Wampler daydreams.

B12

NONFICTION

Far and Away

Check out these wild adventures. Which vacation would you choose to go on?

B19

FICTION

Nori Noom

This science fiction story has a twist to it. Read about Stan and the contest he enters.

B25

NONFICTION

Dive Right In

What's the difference between snorkeling and scuba diving? Find out in this article.

SYNTHESIZING

What a Great Read!

Everyone responds to books differently. Your response is as valuable as anyone else's, but it's important to be able to explain why you feel the way you do. It helps to understand your own thought processes as you form opinions about what you are reading.

Whenever you read a book, you are **synthesizing.** This means that you organize all the different parts of what you are reading in your mind in order to understand the whole text. Synthesizing involves summarizing what you read, but it also involves forming your own personal reaction to the text. Whenever you recommend or criticize a book to a friend, you share just the parts of the book that describe the important events or characters and that support your opinion as a reader. You don't retell every detail of the whole story to your friend.

You can use a two-column Summary/Response chart to better understand the relationship between what you read and how you respond to it. In the example below, Josh describes the content of Lynne Cherry's *The Great Kapok Tree* in the left column and explains how the text created a picture in his mind in the right column.

Summary	Response
In the tropical rain forest of Brazil, a woodsman sleeps before chopping down a giant kapok tree. While he's asleep, all kinds of forest creatures tell him what bad things will happen to them if he chops down the tree. When the woodsman wakes up, the animals and a boy watch to see what he will do. He walks out of the rain forest without chopping down the tree.	The colorful pictures are amazing! The author also created word pictures by using action words like <u>crawled</u>, <u>piped</u>, <u>padded</u>, and <u>growled</u> instead of <u>moved</u> or <u>said</u>. I also liked how she used sound words in sentences like, "The wood of the tree was very hard. . . Whack! Chop! Whack!" And I think the book's message about saving the kapok tree was really strong because she had animals like a tree frog, a jaguar, and a cock-of-the-rock use their own words to explain why the tree was important to them.

By organizing his thinking about *The Great Kapok Tree* in the chart, Josh was able to clearly explain why he liked the book. The next time you encounter a book that you really like—or even one that you don't—use a chart like this one to help you synthesize.

Andy Wampler, Daydreamer

by Mike Graf

"With Orville Wright at the controls, the little airplane bounced across the sandy field. Its engine roared louder, then the plane lifted off the ground and soared up into the sky over Kitty Hawk, North Carolina. It flew for twelve seconds!" Andy held out his arms and swayed from side to side. He could feel the air swooshing by his face as he took off. "Zoom! Zoom! Zoom!"

His teacher, Mrs. Granskog, cleared her throat. "OK, Andy, we get the picture. Please continue with your report."

"Oh yeah," Andy said, stepping back to the podium. "It was December 17, 1903, and Wilbur Wright watched from the ground while his younger brother flew the first successful power-driven airplane with a person on board. The Wright Brothers carried us into the world of technology and aviation, which is why they are considered Great Americans!" Andy took his notes from the podium and looked out at his classmates.

Kaitlyn raised her hand. "Did they ever crash?" she asked.

"Some of their first planes crashed, but they were gliders that flew without engines or people," Andy replied. "But the Wright Brothers never gave up!"

What have you read so far that makes you want to keep on reading? Why?

"That was great, Andy. It sounded like you were really there," said Mrs. Granskog. "Who's next?"

Ben raised his hand.

"OK, Ben."

Andy returned to his seat and relaxed as he watched Ben walk to the front of the room.

Ben turned toward the class. "My book report on Great Americans is about Babe Ruth. He was the most famous baseball player in American history. His real name was George Herman Ruth and he was born in Baltimore, Maryland, in 1895. When he was seven, he was sent to live in an orphanage and learned to play baseball. When he was nineteen, he played for the Baltimore Orioles, and they nicknamed him 'Babe.' Later on, he pitched for the Boston Red Sox. In 1919, Babe Ruth was sold to the New York Yankees and became known for his home run hitting—714 home runs, to be exact!"

Ben lapsed into a monotone voice whenever he was nervous, and today was no exception. As Andy listened, he traveled to Yankee Stadium and heard the announcer: *"And it's Babe Ruth at the plate for what could be one of the last at-bats of his legendary career! Here's the pitch to the Babe. It's swung on . . . a high drive to deep right field! Andy Wampler, the rookie, goes back to the track. To the wall."* Andy raised his arm and jumped way out of his seat. *"He got it!"* the announcer shouted. *"What a sensational play! Wampler takes a home run away from the Babe, and the crowd goes crazy!"*

"Andy? Andy!" Mrs. Granskog was standing next to his desk. "Did you have a question?"

"Huh? Oh no, I apologize. I was just catching a fly," Andy replied and sheepishly slumped back into his seat.

Mrs. Granskog strode back to her desk. "OK, Ben, thank you. Who wants to go next?"

"I will," Jill said. She pranced to the front of the room. "I'm doing my Great Americans report on Rosa Parks. She was an African American who was born in 1913 in Tuskegee, Alabama. Back then, people in the South were prejudiced against black people, and many segregation laws were made. African Americans had to use different drinking fountains and bathrooms than everyone else. Their children had to go to separate schools, and all African Americans had to ride in the back of a bus. And if a white person needed a seat on a crowded bus, black people were supposed to stand up."

"That doesn't sound fair!" Andy cried out.

"I know," Jill agreed. "On December 1, 1955, in Montgomery, Alabama, Rosa Parks got on a bus as usual to go home after work. The bus got crowded and the driver yelled back to Rosa, 'Hey, lady, you're gonna have to stand up so this white gentleman can sit.'"

Now Andy was sitting next to Rosa Parks and could feel the tension on the bus. When he looked over at her, she didn't move. The bus driver became angry. *If you don't get up lady, I'm going to have you arrested!* Andy hopped out of his seat and stood in the aisle with his arms folded across his chest.

Mrs. Granskog took off her glasses. "Andy!"

Andy looked around the room. "Oh, sorry. I just had to stand up for a second."

"The class is sitting quietly and listening to the report." Mrs. Granskog put her glasses back on. "Just like you should be."

"Sorry." Andy quickly plopped back into his seat and folded his arms. He looked up and saw Mrs. Granskog glaring at him. Andy smiled and shrugged his shoulders. "I guess it's hard for me to stay in my seat today. I must have too much 'get up and go.'"

"OK, class," she said, "we have time for one more report before lunch. Sarah, would you like to go next?"

Sarah walked to the front of the room.

Do you have a friend that you think would like this story? Why?

"I'm doing my report on Sacagawea. I can identify with her because I'm part Cherokee. Sacagawea was born in Idaho and was Shoshone. When she was a young girl, Sacagawea was taken to North Dakota. There, she married a fur trader named Toussaint Charbonneau. He was hired by Lewis and Clark in 1804 to come on their yearlong journey across America. Sacagawea also joined the explorers because she was familiar with other Native American tribes and the land. She efficiently helped the explorers interpret native languages, find food, and get across the rivers."

Rivers? Andy thought to himself. He bravely stood on the bank of a raging river with Lewis and Clark. *"How will we ford this river?"* Clark asked Lewis. Sacagawea stepped forward and spoke softly, *"Up farther, the river is narrow. There are many boulders there. We can easily cross."* Andy trotted up the river bank and climbed up on a large rock. Sacagawea and the other explorers followed close behind.

"Andrew Wampler! Get off of my desk!" Mary shouted.

"What?" Andy looked around the room, then down at Mary. She stood with her arms folded, looking up at Andy with a scowl on her face. Next to her was Mrs. Granskog, with her hands perched on her hips.

"Are you wondering what I'm doing up here?" Andy asked.

"I am," Mrs. Granskog replied curtly.

"Well, Mrs. Granskog, being the explorer I am, I discovered tons of spiderwebs hanging off the lights up here and was just checking them out. Sorry." Andy brushed off his hair, hopped down, and sat back down in his seat.

The class watched silently as Mrs. Granskog walked to the back of the room and stood behind Andy. "We have just two minutes left until lunch. Who would like to tell us which Great American they'd like to be and why?"

Andy's hand shot up first.

"OK, Andy," Mrs. Granskog replied. "Tell the class which Great American you'd like to be."

"I'd like to be all of them!"

The children laughed.

"Quiet, class." Mrs. Granskog smiled and strolled to the front of the room. "Why do you say that?"

"Because they're *all* great people!" Andy exclaimed. "Who wouldn't want to fly the first airplane like the Wright Brothers? Hit hundreds of home runs like Babe Ruth? Stand up for your rights like Rosa Parks? And who wouldn't want to be like Sacagawea and explore this great country of ours!"

BRRRING! The lunch bell rang loudly.

"All right, class, you're dismissed for lunch!" Mrs. Granskog returned to her desk. When Andy passed by, she softened her voice and said, "I guess you really *were* listening, weren't you?"

"Of course!" Andy replied.

Mrs. Granskog watched Andy walk out. Then she grabbed her lunch box from her desk. She paused and glanced up at the ceiling to see if there really were spiderwebs. Shaking her head, she flicked off the lights and hurried off to lunch. ⦿

How did the author give you a sense of what kind of person Andy is?

Stop and Respond

Daydream Believer?

Is daydreaming a waste of time, or is it an important part of life? Does daydreaming make you miss out on what's going on around you (like school), or does it help you relax once in a while? In a group, discuss the pros and cons of daydreaming. Assign one person in the group to take notes on your discussion.

Walk in His (or Her) Shoes

What famous person from history would you like to be? Write a story starring you as the hero of an important historical event. In your story, incorporate facts as well as imagination. How did you feel as you faced challenges or made a historical decision?

Armchair Adventure

Some people say that to travel the world, all you need is a bit of imagination—and a great book. Just as Andy Wampler "relives" history by imagining himself there, you can have adventures by imagining that you are the exciting characters in the books you read. Think of an adventure that you would like to take. Now head to the library to find a book about a real person who did it. During the next rainy day, curl up in your favorite chair and read your book. Enjoy your trip!

2. In **Bemidji,** check out statues of Paul Bunyan and his blue ox, "Babe." This was a great lumbering center during the early 1900s.

1. The Mississippi River begins flowing at **Lake Itasca.** Lake Itasca State Park has 3,000 acres of lakes and ponds.

A Mississippi River Adventure

Want to go on an adventure? Travel along the Mississippi River, the largest river in North America. The mighty Mississippi flows south through no fewer than ten states. Here are some places you might want to visit along the way.

3. Laura Ingalls Wilder, author of the beloved *Little House* books, was born in **Pepin, Wisconsin.** A replica of her house sits on the site.

Minnesota
The North Star State

Wisconsin
The Badger State

4. If you like hiking, you can hike to your heart's content at Perrot State Park in **Trempealeau,** where you'll find two 500-foot bluffs to look over the river on.

5. A stop in **Marquette** will allow you to see over 200 prehistoric mounds that have been preserved at Effigy Mounds National Park.

Iowa
The Hawkeye State

6. Pay tribute to the days of pioneers and steamboats at the Buffalo Bill Museum in **LeClaire.**

Illinois
The Land of Lincoln

7. Check out the "Crookedest Street in the World," according to Ripley's Believe It or Not. Snake Alley, in **Burlington,** has five half-curves and two quarter-curves. It drops 58 feet from the top of the road to the bottom, which is 275 feet long.

Missouri
The Show-Me State

8. In **Quincy,** you can stand in Washington Square, where Abraham Lincoln once stood during the famous Lincoln-Douglas debates.

9. The boyhood home of Mark Twain, one of America's most famous authors, still stands in **Hannibal.**

10. In **St. Louis,** visit the St. Louis Arch. This impressive national monument, nicknamed the "Gateway to the West," stands 630 feet tall—more than twice as tall as the Statue of Liberty!

Illinois
The Land of Lincoln

Kentucky
The Bluegrass State

Missouri
The Show-Me State

11. In **Wickliffe,** you'll see an archaeological excavation of a town built by Mississippian Native Americans, who lived there as early as 800 A.D.

Arkansas
The Natural State

13. Spring and fall are popular times to drive through the St. Francis National Forest in **Marianna,** where flowering dogwoods and colorful autumn leaves brighten your path.

Tennessee
The Volunteer State

12. "The Pork Barbecue Capital of the World," "Birthplace of Rock 'n Roll," and "Home of the Blues" all describe **Memphis,** where you can soak up some tunes while eating barbecued pork.

14. The fish are almost always biting at **White River** National Wildlife Refuge, which has 116,000 acres and more than 100 fishing lakes. Try your hand at catching bass, crappie, catfish, and bream.

Mississippi
The Magnolia State

15. Each October, the residents of **Onward** stage a Bear Hunt Reunion in honor of President Theodore Roosevelt. In 1902, Roosevelt refused to shoot a bear while on a hunting trip, inspiring the popular teddy bear toy.

16. At **Vicksburg** National Military Park, you can find artifacts from the U.S.S. Cairo, an ironclad ship sunk by the Confederates during the Civil War. This town's nickname, "Key to Victory," was also the site of many Civil War battles.

Louisiana
The Pelican State

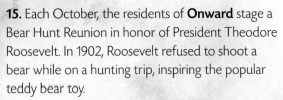

Now that you've seen what the Mississippi River has to offer, create an itinerary for you and a friend as you travel downriver. For more information about other places to visit along the Great River Road, check out www.mississippi-river.com/mrpc.

17. Baton Rouge, Louisiana's capital, is the center of plantation country.

18. Your last stop on the River Road tour will be in **Venice**—where the mighty Mississippi empties into the Gulf of Mexico.

FAR and AWAY

by Patricia J. Murphy

In the dictionary, you'll find the word *remote*. It's an adjective. It means "secluded" or "out-of-the-way." To find your next "remote" vacation spot, read on.

Left: A scarlet Macaw is just one of the amazing animals you'll find in Costa Rica.

A Costa Rican Adventure

Deep in the thicket of Central America's Costa Rican rain forests, nature lovers will discover a tropical wilderness unmatched by any other in the world. Did you know that 27% of Costa Rica is protected? That is, nearly a third of Costa Rica has been set aside as national parks or private, protected reserves.

In Costa Rica, you'll discover some of the most unexplored terrain in the world. So, to get where you'll be going, you'll travel by air, by boat, and by foot. Bring plenty of bug spray and comfy shoes. Your vacation might include one of the following Costa Rican adventures.

- Explore the ancient trees, lowland forest layers, rivers, beaches, and swamps of Costa Rica's Corcovado National Park. You'll spy scarlet macaws, mangrove blackhawks, tapir, anteaters, cougars, ocelots, howler and spider monkeys, frogs of all kinds, and more—all by foot or by paddleboat!

- View the Cloud Forest Preserve of Monteverde as you hum along with the hummingbirds and grab a seat next to a resting Blue Morpho butterfly.

- Get up close and personal (but not too close!) with Costa Rica's Arenal Volcano, which erupted in 1968. It's famous for its loud rumbling noises, bursts of smoke, and erupting lava!
- Swim, fish, snorkel, or dive along Costa Rica's Tamarindo Beach on the Pacific coast. Later, if you have the energy, get on a horse and venture off to a beach where the giant leatherback turtles nest!

For forests of information on Costa Rica, log onto www.odci.gov/cia/publications/factbook/geos/cs.html.

Cool, Dude!

No, you don't have to be a dude to visit a Montana dude ranch, but you do have to have a sense of cowboy (or cowgirl) adventure! Some dude ranches in Montana are just "a hoot and a holler" from the majestic Glacier National Park and next to the Flathead National Forest. You can saddle up your horse and gallop on the slopes of the Continental Divide for the ride of a lifetime. Hold on to the reins as you:

- Get to work. Ranch guests can mend fences, haul heavy loads, gather stray cattle, and drive a herd from one place to another in a real cattle round-up.

- Relax—well, not really. At some dude ranches, the word is "no work and all play will make you the last in line for supper." (And you DO NOT want to be last in line!)
- Devour hearty, wholesome vittles—Montana barbecue style—made by "real" cowboys.

> Which place so far would you like to visit most? Why?

- Enjoy moonlight hayrides, lively square dancing, and scary ghost stories told around a fire. But beware! Some of the stories may frighten you out of your spurs, leaving you terrorized and shaking in your cowboy boots!

To rope up more information about a dude ranch getaway, check out www.montanadra.com/dude

Lasso yourself some fun as you take a trip to a dude ranch.

The cold temperatures of the South Pole don't seem to bother this penguin.

South Pole or Bust

Don't mind cold temperatures, fierce winds, snow, ice, and dryness? Then a trip to the coldest, driest, and windiest place in the world may be just right for you. Enjoy an expedition to the most remote points of the South Pole (and maybe on Earth). Follow in the tracks of other famous explorers who traveled there decades before you! Here are the chilling details.

● Travel aboard a landing craft that will allow you and fellow Antarctica explorers the chance to see remote beaches along the Antarctica Peninsula, the Falkland Islands, and the South Shetland Islands.

● Bask in the continuous daylight for as long as your sunscreen holds out! (And perhaps bring some blinders to wear at night.)

● See rugged mountains and larger-than-life icebergs in different shapes, sizes, and colors. Don't forget the white glaciers and ice floes, either!

● Waddle close to penguins, seabirds, and seals. Even see a few blue whales.

● Check out Antarctica's Scientific Research Stations and meet their station members. Get the scoop on their current polar and oceanographic discoveries.

● Learn everything you've ever wanted to know about Antarctica and more from your expedition leaders—like how to keep warm, dry, and alive, for starters.

To warm up to more information on Antarctica, check out www.secretsoftheice.org.

Tanzanian Safari

Did somebody say "safari"? Join fellow safari friends, a knowledgeable driver, and a guide for a wild time exploring wildlife in Tanzania, Africa. Here's what you and your extremely brave safari friends can expect on your Tanzanian Safari.

● Travel along rugged plains by jeep and by foot! Take a plane to the smaller, even more remote areas of the "bush," if you're game!

● Stay as close to the animals as safety will allow in a covered tent that has a bedroom AND a bathroom.

- Satisfy your appetite with a safari sunrise breakfast, light afternoon lunch, and dinner prepared by your safari chef amidst a Tanzanian sunset. Sample local coffee, area delicacies such as goat's meat and cow hooves, and specially flown-in entrees from around the globe!
- See large herds of elephants—up to 300 at a time—at the Tarangire National Park. (Make sure to bring fast action film! These animals don't stop for pictures!)
- Drive to the Ngorongoro Crater and view the largest East African population of lion, elephant, hyena, wildebeest, and endangered black rhino.
- Sit beside a glowing campfire and listen to old and new African stories, tales, and legends. Gaze at the stars and watch the nocturnal animals awaken to start their days!
- Finish the safari with a side trip to Spice Island in Zanzibar, where you can snorkel, bike, and enjoy white sandy beaches.

For more wild information about Tanzania, visit www.tanzania-web.com or www.geographia.com/tanzania.

The wildebeest (right) is only one of the exotic animals you can see at the Serengeti National Park in Tanzania.

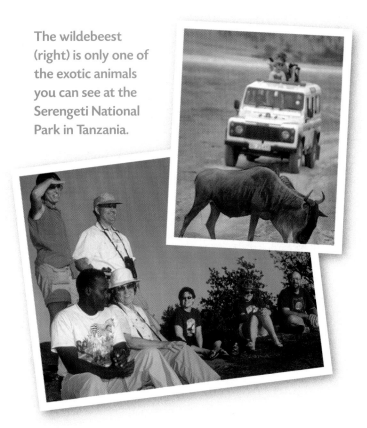

This might be the reason it's called Kangaroo Island.

A Hop to Kangaroo Island

G'day, mates! Come join us on Kangaroo Island in the land down under. You may get tired hopping around this magnificent island that's 700 miles due west of Sydney, Australia, but you'll never grow tired of its endless natural wonders. Each day on Kangaroo Island can be as wild or as tame as you'd like!

- Explore the 1,679 square miles of Kangaroo Island by four-wheel drive, and surround yourself with the island's residents including sea lions, emus, wallabies, koalas, platypus, and of course, kangaroos!
- Visit Seal Bay and its 600 rare sea lions.
- Journey through Flinders Chase National Park where you'll see koalas, kangaroos, wallabies, and Australian birds including pelicans, bush turkeys, and rare glossy black cockatoos!
- Make new friends at the Parndana Wildlife Park—a special reserve for orphaned kangaroos, koalas, and other Australian animals that need mothering.

Is there someone you know that would especially enjoy one of these remote vacations?

- Watch the sheep being milked at a local sheep dairy, and taste freshly made cheeses and yogurts.
- Go little penguin watching! Beginning at dusk, hit the beaches to see the island's little penguins return to the shores to feed their young with the catch of the day. Standing only 12 inches tall (thus earning them the "little" name), the little penguins make their homes on the island's cliffs and hills.

For more information about Australia and Kangaroo Island, hop on the Internet at www.gigglepotz.com/caustralia.htm or www.webweaver.com.au/australia.

Galloping Galapagos!

Sea lions that swim with you. Butterflies that can't get close enough to you. Animal species that don't fear humans. Sound too good to be true? Not on the Galapagos Islands, 600 miles off the coast of Ecuador! Formed five million years ago from volcanic activity, what was left behind is a harsh terrain and wildlife seen nowhere else in the world. As a Galapagos Islands traveler, you will:

- Get wet—not just a little, but a whole lot—when you land on the islands in a small boat or dinghy called a *panga*. (Sorry, no hotel towels to dry off with!)
- Explore the island's white sandy beaches in a kayak and hike close to animals you'll never see anywhere else in the world. These animals include the waved albatross, Hood mockingbird, Sally Light-foot crab, Galapagos penguins, and blue-footed boobies.
- Watch the flamingoes feeding in a large lagoon.
- Snorkel and discover the Galapagos Islands' fantastic underwater landscape that includes sea lions and green turtles!

For more islands of information on the Galapagos Islands, check out www.wwf.org/galapagos.

Need more ideas to plan your remote vacation? Why not use one from Ralph Waldo Emerson? "Do not go where the path may lead," said Emerson. "Go instead where there is no path and leave a trail."

If you follow Emerson's advice, we guarantee that you won't come back the same way you left. Sure, you may come home with mounds of dirty laundry and a sunburn (or windburn), but that's on the outside. We're talking about your inside, and the memories to cherish.

By going away—far away—and leaving behind the ordinary in search of the extraordinary, by losing the remote control and finding the remotest areas of the planet, you'll experience a whole new world—and a whole new you. And THAT you can't find in any dictionary! ◯

> Think of a few things about each remote place that you would enjoy and not enjoy doing or seeing.

A *panga* (above) will get you up close to the action on the Galapagos Islands.

Stop and Respond

Mix and Match

How well do you know your classmates? In this activity, work with a partner and reread the article with your partner's personality in mind. Which adventure would he or she like best? Which one does your partner think you will like best? Come up with reasons for your choices and share your opinions with your partner. How well did you do in choosing an adventure for your partner?

The Ultimate Adventure

What would be the ultimate adventure for you? Maybe it's white-water rafting, catching a giant marlin, or climbing Mt. Everest. How do you see yourself overcoming the challenges you face? Create a comic strip that shows you in your glory.

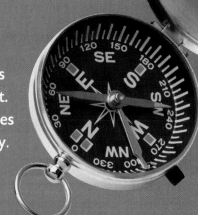

When Life Gives You Lemons...

Make lemonade! It's important to make the most of unexpected situations, especially during a vacation. In a group, take turns role-playing how you would react if: a) it rained during your beach vacation, b) you got poison ivy during a camping trip, or c) no one spoke English in the town you were visiting. Use your imaginations to come up with other unexpected situations and explain how you'd deal with them.

SYNTHESIZING

The Australian Outback

When you're reading to gather factual information, it helps to be aware of your thinking process as you **synthesize** the text. As you read, you gradually form an opinion about the text. This opinion helps you to decide whether you will need to read more books to get the information you are looking for.

Sarah looked up information on the Internet about living in the Australian Outback. She found a Web site written by a person who lives there. Here's part of the site that deals with living in the Outback.

> The vast distances on the Australian Outback have forced people to adapt to their isolation. After all, some people are more than a day's drive to their nearest neighbor—not a very convenient distance for borrowing a cup of sugar! Therefore, a two-way radio and an airstrip are vital to any Outback station, or ranch.
>
> Because of the great distances, some children in the Outback cannot attend regular school. They learn from the School of the Air, a special school where the teacher and student interact via a two-way radio.

As Sarah read the text, she recorded her thoughts about what she'd read. As you can see, some of the information was useful, but Sarah decided she wanted more details.

Facts I Discovered	My Thoughts	Author's Description
• People have to drive for more than a day to visit neighbors!	• I'd be bored if I lived that far away from neighbors.	• The word "isolation" makes me feel lonely.
• Children use a two-way radio to "go to school."	• I wouldn't like this kind of school. I'd miss playing with friends. How do they hand in assignments?	• I wish the writer gave more information about this type of school. "Special school" doesn't say much!

Try using a chart like this one the next time you're reading a text for information. It will help you see the relationship between the way an author presents facts and your reaction to what you've read.

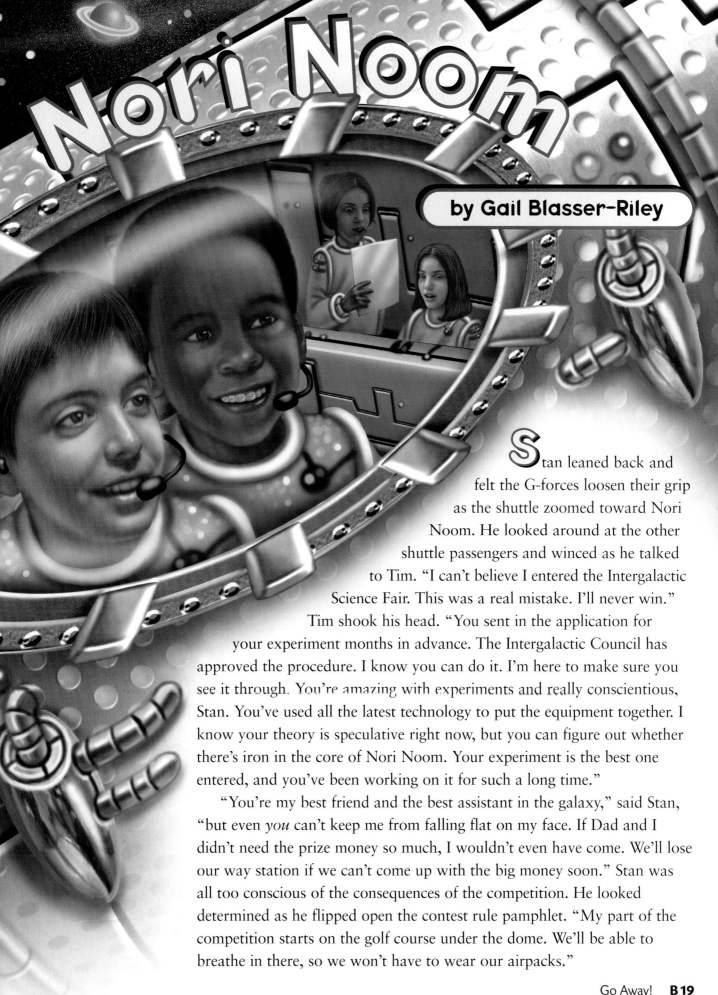

Nori Noom

by Gail Blasser-Riley

Stan leaned back and felt the G-forces loosen their grip as the shuttle zoomed toward Nori Noom. He looked around at the other shuttle passengers and winced as he talked to Tim. "I can't believe I entered the Intergalactic Science Fair. This was a real mistake. I'll never win."

Tim shook his head. "You sent in the application for your experiment months in advance. The Intergalactic Council has approved the procedure. I know you can do it. I'm here to make sure you see it through. You're amazing with experiments and really conscientious, Stan. You've used all the latest technology to put the equipment together. I know your theory is speculative right now, but you can figure out whether there's iron in the core of Nori Noom. Your experiment is the best one entered, and you've been working on it for such a long time."

"You're my best friend and the best assistant in the galaxy," said Stan, "but even *you* can't keep me from falling flat on my face. If Dad and I didn't need the prize money so much, I wouldn't even have come. We'll lose our way station if we can't come up with the big money soon." Stan was all too conscious of the consequences of the competition. He looked determined as he flipped open the contest rule pamphlet. "My part of the competition starts on the golf course under the dome. We'll be able to breathe in there, so we won't have to wear our airpacks."

"But how will we find the site the council has set aside for your experiment?" asked Tim. "Where are all the other contestants starting? And where are we supposed to look for the clues?"

"On the golf course," Stan said. "The pamphlet says everyone's clues will be hidden on the golf course. I'm guessing we'll have to go through the tunnel to the outside. We'd better hang on to our airpacks, just in case."

"Well, I'm great at figuring out clues," said Tim. "This should be a piece of intergalactic cake!"

"I'm not so worried about finding the clues," said Stan. "But what happens if it takes us too long to find the site they've set up for my experiment? We'll only have ten minutes after the sirens sound to finish everything." Stan hung his head. "You know I don't like to be rushed. I'll probably lose. Maybe this whole trip was a mistake."

"You're being negative, Stan," said Tim. He smiled, and his star-shaped braces caught the light filtering in through the shuttle window. "Amazing what a case of nerves can do to a guy! Did you leave your confidence back at home?"

Stan knew that Tim didn't have much interest in science. He knew, though, that Tim would be pushing him to forge ahead and win because he was the most positive friend in the world. Tim always said that he hated it when Stan doubted himself.

The shuttle finally landed. Tim dashed across the bridge. His weighted shoes kept his steps even. "Stan!" he called back. "Coming?"

Stan yelled, "Affirmative," and raced across the bridge to catch up to his friend. The banner draped across the front of the course caught his attention: NORI NOOM COMPETITION 3000. He looked out through the top of the clear dome.

Billions of tiny stars sent light showers toward them. The stars pierced pinholes through the intergalactic darkness. Stan pulled in a deep gulp of dome air. The delicate aroma of roses filled his senses. He knew the fragrance came from a bush loved by his ancestors, a bush that could never grow outside in the arid Nori Noom atmosphere. Nothing could grow here.

How would you explain the story to a friend so far?

"Stan, Nori Noom to Stan. Stan, come in. Beep, beep, beep!" Tim said in a monotone.

Stan realized he'd been unconsciously staring off into space, as if he were in a trance. He was imagining what would happen if he actually had time to play a round of golf. In this atmosphere, one small thwack of the club would send the ball looping and sailing.

"Look over there," Tim said, pointing west. Stan saw a piece of paper taped on a door! EULC: OG HGUORHT EREH. He wasn't sure what it meant, but he figured it was probably some sort of clue. His investigative nature kicked in. He had to take a look. "I think it's calling us, Stan," said Tim. "I don't think you can win the competition under the dome. A few small steps through this door, down the tunnel, and we'll be outside. You'll be able to get to work."

"What's the use?" asked Stan. "I won't win." He shook like the wing of a space shuttle entering Earth's atmosphere.

"Stan, you have enough gray matter between your ears to build a galaxy, but you act like you don't even have enough inside your noggin to make a tiny gray crayon."

Stan had to smile. Tim sometimes got carried away, but it was one of the things Stan really liked about his friend.

"What'll it be?" asked Tim. "What are you thinking? Could you be a bit more communicative?" Tim blew a tiny lightning gub

How do you feel about Stan and Tim? Are they like you or not? How?

out of the way. "These things are so pesky," he said. "I don't know why they can't keep them out from under the dome."

Stan reached for the door handle. He wasn't looking forward to leaving the dome. The air outside was atrocious. It smelled like gases and ether. And the lightning gubs were thick, as thick as the flies Stan's ancestors had written about in accounts of Earth picnics from long ago. You had to push aside the gubs to get anywhere. Still, Stan decided to try to move forward. He motioned to Tim. The two set off down the tunnel as they pulled their airpacks and helmets out of their backpacks.

Stan listened to the echo of their footsteps as they walked. The echo faded gradually, like the sound of a siren that blares and then sounds fainter and fainter until it finally fades away.

There was another door at the end of the tunnel. Before Stan gave the door a shove, the two friends popped on their airpacks and helmets. Stan looked at Tim through his faceplate, turned on his microphone, and watched as the door slowly opened. His knees knocked so hard, Stan thought they must have sounded like drums. "Who am I kidding?" he huffed to Tim, as he shoved aside a huge swarm of lightning gubs. "There's no way I'll do this in time. I might as well kiss the way station good-bye."

"At least let's look for another clue," said Tim. He patted Stan on the back. "You can do that much."

The clue wasn't far away. Stan saw a huge, wooden red arrow planted in the soil. A single word on the arrow read: EULC. "I'm not sure what that means," he said, pulling the digital direction finder from his pocket and punching in the variables. "But the arrow is pointing toward Nori Mount. According to my map, that's at the center of Nori Noom, and it'd be the perfect place for the council to choose for the experiments. It's just a quarter-mile away. Maybe we'll be the first ones there!"

Stan adjusted the weights in his boots so he could move more swiftly. Tim did the same. They looped and spun their way to Nori Mount. EULC: EREH the sign read. Stan wasn't sure what it meant, but thought he must be in the right place. He pulled off his backpack and exerted almost all his energy to set up his equipment. Little wells of sweat sprung up all across his forehead. Lightning gubs swarmed around his equipment.

As Stan worked, he heard the sirens. "The sirens!" He gasped. "We only have ten minutes to finish. Stop shaking!" he shouted to his hands. "We have to work fast. If I can come up with an iron reading on the digitized meter, I'll win. No one will ever be able to take our family way station away—not in a decade, not in a monomillennium!"

Swiftly, Stan sunk the probe into the dusty soil. The round symbols on his meter formed a pyramid that pointed right to the iron section. "It's iron!" he cried. "The core of Nori Noom is iron!"

Just then, the mirror on the readout for Stan's probe caught the Nori Noom Mount sign. Stan's jaw dropped. The letters appeared backward in his mirror. "Iron Moon!" he shouted. "The clue was there all along. ALL of the clues were there all along!"

As the judges raced to his side, Stan motioned to his meter. His jaws almost ached from his wide smile. He jotted down his results and demonstrated his experiment to the judges.

He'd done what he'd come to Nori Noom to do.

Would you recommend this story to a friend? Why or why not?

Stop and Respond

Work in Progress

In a group, brainstorm a place with an odd feature, like the backwardness of Nori Noom. Work out the setting, plot, and main characters for a story set there. When you all agree on the story's direction, work together to create a storyboard to share with the class. Have the class vote on the best storyboard and then work together to write it.

N is for "Not Usual"

Nori Noom is an unusual place, with a name that provides a clue to what it's like. Write a poem about this place by writing each letter of Nori Noom down the left side of a large piece of paper. For each letter in the name, write a sentence that describes this backward place.

SEULC

At what point in the story did you figure out that Nori Noom meant "Iron Moon" spelled backward? What parts of the text gave you hints or clues? Make a list and share it with a partner.

Dive Right In

by Lisa Rao

Have you ever gazed into a sparkling ocean and wondered about the fascinating creatures beneath its surface? Perhaps you've seen TV specials about dolphins, coral reefs, or sea turtles, and wished you could experience them up close and personal. In this article, you'll read about two exciting ways to explore the undersea world. Are you ready? On your mark, get set . . . go!

Take the Plunge: Snorkel!

Snorkeling is the simplest method of underwater exploration. You don't need much equipment and you can learn without any lessons. The most difficult part is getting used to breathing through a snorkel. Otherwise, if you can swim, you're well on your way.

Snorkeling, in its most basic form, requires only three pieces of equipment: a mask, a snorkel, and swimming fins. The diving mask covers your nose and eyes, enabling you to see while underwater. The snorkel is a tube that allows you to breathe while floating near the water's surface. One end fits into your mouth and the other end extends above the water. Finally, on your feet you wear swimming fins. They make your feet look like a large duck's feet! Fins help propel you through the water.

Once your equipment is on, it's easier to start with just your face submerged in the water, breathing through the snorkel. As you feel more comfortable, take a deep breath, hold it, and dive under the water. Some snorkelers can hold their breath for nearly three minutes.

One of the most important skills to learn about snorkeling is to be able to clear your snorkel when it becomes filled with water. Some snorkels already have a built-in device that automatically removes any water. But if you use an older model snorkel, you have to practice blowing out the water on your own before breathing in again. This takes practice.

What makes snorkeling something you would or would not want to try?

"The main thing is to stay calm," says Suki York, an experienced snorkeler. "When you put your face in the water, remember not to open your mouth. Simply breathe through your snorkel. If you get any water in your snorkel, just exhale (blow) really hard to clear it. Most people get nervous if water gets in their snorkel, and that only makes the problem worse, because then they forget the rules and open their mouth, and end up swallowing even more water!"

Snorkeling is an inexpensive way to discover underwater life. Many places will rent a mask, fins, and a snorkel for about six dollars a day. So give it a try on your next vacation!

SCUBA:
A Whole Different World

The word SCUBA is an acronym. Each letter stands for another word: **S**elf-**C**ontained **U**nderwater **B**reathing **A**pparatus.

Scuba diving is very different from snorkeling. While snorkeling only requires three pieces of equipment, scuba diving requires a tank of air, a regulator, a weight belt, and a buoyancy compensator vest. In order to keep warm, scuba divers must also wear either a wet suit or a dry suit. Wet suits are usually worn in warm-water climates like Hawaii. A dry suit is worn in areas where water temperatures drop below 50 degrees Fahrenheit. It keeps a diver completely dry.

Scuba diving should always be practiced with at least one other person—a dive buddy. Dive buddies learn to double-check each other's equipment and help each other out in case of a problem. Because you can't speak underwater, divers also learn how to communicate using hand signals.

If you decide you want to scuba dive often, you should get certified. There are different levels of certification, but most often you complete five pool dives and five open water dives with an instructor before you are certified. Once you are certified, you can scuba dive without professional supervision.

Many scuba divers today dive with computers that help them determine safe diving depths. At deeper depths, "The sea life becomes much more dramatic," Marc Chamberlain, a diver and underwater photographer, says. "Scuba diving is better (than snorkeling) for underwater photography, since the photographer needs plenty of time underwater to set up shots, position lights and cameras, etc."

Unlike snorkeling, scuba equipment and lessons can be expensive. To rent scuba equipment for one day, it may cost you nearly one hundred dollars. The view below might be worth the extra money, however.

> What makes scuba diving something you would or would not want to try?

Life Below the Surface

A visit to a coral reef is a real treat! Snorkeling just below the surface will introduce you to a whole new world. You can see schools of bright orange clownfish as well as angelfish, spotted stingrays, rainbow-colored sea urchins, and anemones. It's important to remember that a coral reef is alive—so do not break off a piece of coral as a souvenir. It is against the law. "Look, but don't touch" is the rule to go by. If you visit some of the bigger reefs in Florida or in Hawaii, you can usually buy a little packet of fish food to feed your new friends. And you will make several—very quickly! These fish look forward to being fed by tourists like you!

Should you ever become a scuba diver, there are even more extraordinary things to explore the further down you go. The deeper you go, the less light there is. The sea creatures that live further down in the ocean have found ways to see and be seen in the watery depths. Some fish, such as the lanternfish, glow in the dark. Another fish, the deep-sea hachet, has glowing patches on its lips. Unsuspecting smaller fish are lead right into its hungry mouth!

People have always been fascinated by the ocean. Because of inventions such as snorkels and scuba gear, we are able to explore the underwater world. According to the Professional Association of Dive Instructors (PADI), there are approximately 6 million active divers around the world today. Perhaps sometime soon you, too, will be one of them!

> How did the author peak your interest about undersea diving?

Fun Fact

If you're a girl, here's some good news: you have an advantage over boys when it comes to snorkeling. "Boys usually have more muscle tone and their bodies are heavier," says Suki York. "Girls have less muscle and are usually lighter, so it's easier for them to simply float close to the surface and snorkel. For boys this takes more practice, since they're heavier."

SCUBA vs. Snorkeling

Chances are you weren't aware of the differences between scuba diving and snorkeling. A great way to be sure you understand the differences between two things that seem alike is to create a Venn Diagram. On a sheet of paper, draw two circles that overlap in the middle. In the left circle, list characteristics of snorkeling that are different from those of scuba diving. In the right circle, list the unique characteristics of scuba diving. Where the two circles overlap, list characteristics that both sports have in common. Based on your chart, decide which sport you would prefer, and why.

Deep Sea Gallery

Find or copy some pictures of the unusual creatures that live far below the ocean's surface. Some of these animals are mentioned in "Dive Right In," but there are many more amazing creatures to discover. With your classmates, design an exhibit that shows the many adaptations deep-sea fish have made to their dark underwater world.

Diver's Delights

Where would you like to snorkel or scuba dive? Perhaps it's the Great Barrier Reef in Australia, the Florida Keys, or even a local lake. Find out about the animals and plants that live in that aquatic environment. Create a poster of the wildlife you might see during your underwater adventure.

Let's Write

Destination: Fantasy Vacation

What's your ideal vacation spot—a deserted tropical beach? a wooded mountaintop? a colorful and noisy city? Think about details that would make such a place the perfect setting for escaping your busy life. Use these details to create a travel brochure about your ideal vacation. Cut out pictures from old magazines and write descriptive text that shows why this location is the perfect place for a fantasy vacation.

Be the Teacher

Think of an activity that you really like doing, such as sailing, fishing, or ice-skating. Write a brief article explaining your hobby to your classmates, much like the author of "Dive Right In" did. Include information about how to learn the basics of the skill, the materials required, and the best places to practice it. If possible, include a photograph of you performing the activity. Share your illustrated article with the class.

A Get-Away Party

Can't go on a real vacation? Then go on a pretend one! Create invitations to a party with your favorite vacation theme. In your invitations, mention what people should wear, the props they should bring, and provide hints about how you would decorate to create a real-life setting. Your invitation could take the form of a rhymed poem, a formal letter, or anything else you think is appropriate.

More Books

Boettner, John S. *Hey Mom, Can I Ride My Bike Across America?: Five Kids Meet Their Country.* Sbf Productions, 1990.

James, Dan. *Jack's Time Machine.* Troll Communications, 2000.

Ross, Michael Elsohn. *The Happy Camper Handbook: A Guide for Kids and Their Parents.* Yosemite Association, 1995.

On the Web

Travel Writers Tell All
http://www.rice.edu/projects/topics/travel/
pages.htm

Say "Hello" to the World
http://www.ipl.org/youth/hello/others.html

A Virtual Tour of the Universe
http://library.thinkquest.org/28327/main/
cockpit.html

Across the Curriculum

Social Studies

Experienced travelers know that they'll have a much better time visiting other countries if they arrive prepared. They learn as much as possible about the country's culture, customs, and history. Imagine that you are about to visit a faraway land. Create a fact sheet that includes important information, such as local foods to try, common sayings, important historical dates, and major land or water forms. Organize your information so that it's easy to read at a glance.

Math

Whether you're planning a trip to an exotic location or a simple backpacking trip, it's important to have an idea of what your vacation will cost. Create a budget for a trip you might take with a friend. Think of all the expenses, such as transportation, lodging, food, entrance fees, and entertainment. How much will your trip cost? Which category costs the most money? Which costs the least? Finally, try to trim your budget to get rid of unnecessary expenses.

Vacationing in Your Backyard

Want to help your parents feel like kids again? Pitch a tent in your backyard! Backyard camping has lots of advantages, such as running water, convenient bathrooms, and a nearby kitchen. Plus, just like at a real campsite, you can roast marshmallows, catch lightning bugs, and tell ghost stories. And the best part of backyard camping is that you can always run home to get anything you forgot.

Just like camping anywhere else, you'll need certain supplies. Here's a list of things you shouldn't "leave home" without.

✓ **Tent:** Set up a tent in the backyard or make a tent out of some old blankets.

✓ **Warm Clothes:** Whether it's sweatpants or flannel PJs, you want to be sure that everyone is dressed warmly. Don't let sudden drops in temperature catch you off guard. Fashion is definitely NOT important on camping trips!

✓ **Food:** Pack tasty food for your adventure. Tell your parents not to fill up on sweets (or you'll never get them to sleep). Decide beforehand whether you'll eat breakfast at "camp" or at home, and pack accordingly.

✓ **Grill:** Bring a small barbecue grill (setting up the grill and lighting it is definitely a chore for your parents). A grill is the next best thing to a campfire for keeping you warm, roasting marshmallows, and telling spooky stories around.

✓ **Bug Spray:** Don't let the mosquitoes ruin your camping trip. Use bug spray, and don't forget—always zip up your tent whenever you enter or leave it. There's nothing like the buzz of a mosquito to ruin your sleep.

✓ **Activities:** Before camping, get a book about constellations from the library. At nightfall, break out the telescope if you have one—or a pair of binoculars—and explore the stars.

Once you've set up camp and planned the evening's activities, you're all set. Although you might feel safe in your own backyard, you might leave the backdoor unlocked—just in case your parents get scared and want to end the adventure a little early.

COMPREHENSION QUARTERLY

CQ

5

ISSUE C: Inferring

KEEPING YOUR BALANCE

Keeping Your Balance

THINK ABOUT: Inferring

C4

FICTION
Fighting for the Frogs
A field trip results in some very interesting discoveries.

C11

NONFICTION
A Balancing Act
Five kids talk about how balance affects the sports they play.

C19

FICTION
Like Clockwork
Always late for something? Read how one boy solves this problem.

C25

NONFICTION
Success for Preteens
Here's a simple recipe to help relieve your stress.

In this issue:

INFERRING

Giving It Your All

"Is that a good book?" asked Mitch.

Tony looked up at his friend. "Yeah, it is. It's about a kid named Hank who wants to be an Olympic swimmer."

"Do you think he'll make it?"

"He might. He's sure working hard enough at it. All he can think about is swimming. There's nothing else in his life."

"Maybe that's the way he wants it," commented Mitch.

"Maybe, but everyone doesn't feel the same way. Hank's teacher is upset because he's always tired in class. His best friend thinks he's getting stuck-up because he's won a few medals." Tony paused. "You know, I understand how Hank feels. I remember how hard I worked when I wanted to make the All-Star baseball team. But I can see why his teacher and his friend are upset with him, too. I guess I really don't think it's such a good idea to make one thing so important to you."

"Well, let me know how it ends," said Mitch.

"I will." Tony went back to his reading.

As Tony reads, he combines his own experiences with the text to create a meaning that is personal and meaningful. He thinks about how each of the characters in the story feels and is able to consider things from their unique viewpoints.

Like Tony, good readers **infer**, or create meanings that are not directly stated in the text. They interpret meaning by combining what they already know with what they read.

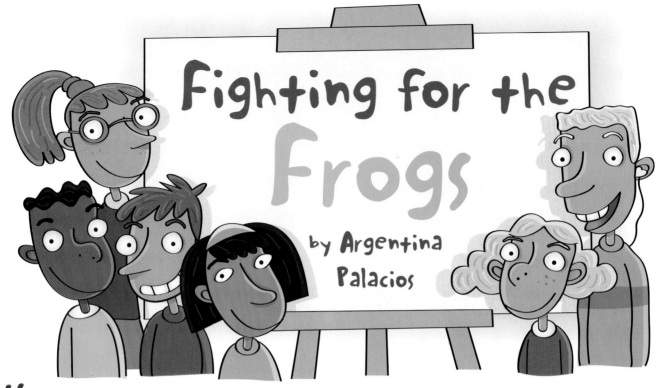

Fighting for the Frogs

by Argentina Palacios

"No one would have imagined at the beginning of the school year that our fifth-grade class would be here today," Pete began. "We have been invited to speak at this convention of Farmers and Ranchers of the Future because of a discovery we made on a field trip. It all started back in September. I remember we were making jokes about frogs, but what we discovered was no joking matter."

"Today we are going to start a unit about frogs," said Ms. Price. "Who knows something about frogs that you could share?"

Pete said, "I know a good joke about frogs!"

Marcy giggled. "So do I."

Ms. Price hesitated. "All right, we can start with some jokes. Tell us yours, Pete."

"What does a well-dressed frog wear?" asked Pete.

"What?" someone answered.

"A jumpsuit!" replied Pete, and everybody laughed.

"My turn," said Marcy. "In a restaurant, a patron asked the waiter, 'Do you have frog legs?' and the waiter answered, 'No, I always walk this way.'"

"Mine is better," said Carlos. "What's a frog's favorite time?"

"I give up. What?" asked Greg.

"Leap year! Ha ha ha!"

We would have gone on with the jokes, but Ms. Price said it was time to start the lesson.

"Frogs, toads, and salamanders are amphibians," Ms. Price said. "Amphibians are found in all the continents, except Antarctica. Amphibians are ancient animals that have been around for about 360 million years. The word *amphibian* means "double life" because these animals live part of their lives in water and part of their lives on land."

Ms. Price then told us we were going on a field trip to a pond on a

> What would you infer about the personalities of the students and teacher so far?

nearby farm. There were lots of frogs in that pond. "When we go to the pond," she said, "I want you to think like scientists. The first thing a scientist does is observe. Scientists always carry a notebook to record what they see."

When we went to the pond, Greg caught the first frog. "Weird!" he exclaimed when he realized that the frog he was holding had only one leg instead of two.

At first the other kids accused Greg of injuring the frog when he caught it, but soon a lot of us had caught other abnormal-looking frogs. About half of the frogs caught that day had deformities or abnormalities. Some had extra legs. Some had only one eye.

We wrote everything we saw in our notebooks. It was not pretty. Besides the strange-looking frogs, we found picnic leftovers and empty insect repellent containers. In the weeks and months following that field trip, we went back to the pond many times. It was through our studies that Project Frog Care was born.

Ms. Price contacted the wildlife authorities. Local scientists began to pay close attention to what we had found. We worked with other researchers and learned about problems facing amphibians in general, and frogs in particular, throughout the rest of the world. Then we shared our findings with TV, radio, and newspaper reporters.

Make an inference: How did the students' attitude about frogs change?

"And that's how we got here today. Some of us would like to take this opportunity to tell you what we learned," Pete said.

"Frogs have been around since before the dinosaurs. They have been able to survive both climatic and geological changes on Earth when

Caught 11 frogs
2 had only one leg
1 had three legs
2 had only one eye
1 was missing a foot
5 looked OK

other animals could not. But now their future looks bleak. People may have caused some of the problems frogs face today by upsetting nature's delicate balance, but we are also the ones that might be able to save them.

"Scientists have noticed and reported frogs with deformities for a long time—about 200 years. But those reports were rare.

"In the last 20 years or so, reports of deformed and abnormal frogs have become quite frequent. And the numbers of such animals are very high. Just to illustrate the point, all the students who will speak to you today have had first-hand experience with this problem.

"Last fall on our field trip, we found dozens and dozens of the strangest-looking frogs you can imagine—legs missing and extra legs. I remember one had a leg growing from its mouth. It was strange—even scary.

"And you know what? Frogs like these are found in great numbers in most states of the U.S., several provinces in Canada, and parts of Mexico—that is, all over North America. There are reports of similar problems in countries as far away as Australia."

Lelia spoke next. "Some scientists who study frogs believe that chemical fertilizers and pesticides that are used on farms may cause the deformities and abnormalities that Pete spoke about," she began. "Pesticides kill the insects that destroy crops, but when it rains, the chemicals eventually find their way into rivers, creeks, and ponds.

"Frogs have permeable skin. That means that they absorb air through their skin. They may live on land, but they require moisture in order to survive. Also, frogs lay their eggs in the water. These eggs don't have a hard shell; they are like gelatin and can absorb contaminants from the water.

"When frogs hatch into tadpoles, they go through a series of changes called *metamorphosis* to become frogs. They have

Why care about frogs?

Antibiotics

Pest control

Painkillers

to stay in the water until they're fully grown, continually absorbing more water through their skin. That's why some scientists believe that chemical pollution is affecting the frogs."

"Other scientists have different theories that explain why there are so many deformed and abnormal frogs," Marcy explained. "One is the hypothesis of *predation,* which means that one member of a species preys on other animals in its own species. One such case is the African clawed frog, which has been introduced in other parts of the world outside its native habitat. This frog has been known to eat a whole frog or just part of one.

"Another hypothesis is that an excessive amount of ultraviolet rays from the sun has had an effect on frogs. In lab experiments, batches of frog eggs were exposed to heavy amounts of ultraviolet radiation for a certain period of time. When the eggs hatched and the tadpoles developed into frogs, many were deformed. If this also happens in the wild, it may very well be because the ozone layer is thinning, causing more exposure to these ultraviolet rays."

It was Sandra's turn. "The problem facing frogs is not only about deformities and abnormalities. There are entire species of frogs vanishing from the face of the earth. Many frogs disappear because the wetlands where they once lived have been destroyed.

In what ways that affect frogs have people upset nature's balance?

"Why should we care about frogs? The list of reasons is long. Just let me say that some antibiotics and painkillers have been developed after studying the substances frogs produce in order to protect themselves. Some medications to treat wounds, certain forms of cancer, and stomach disorders also come from frogs. Just yesterday I learned that scientists are experimenting with a substance derived from the African clawed frog. They are using it to treat a very rare bone disorder that affects some children."

Greg took over the microphone next. "Frogs are also pest control agents—they eat tons of insects—insects that can destroy crops and carry diseases. If there were more frogs around, we might not need to depend so much on chemical pesticides.

What you can do

Call your state environmental office

Visit Web sites

"Long ago, people used to send canaries into mines to make sure the air was safe for the miners. If the canary came back, the miners went in. If the canary didn't come back, it was because it had died, so the miners wouldn't enter the mine. Well, frogs could be helping us like the canaries did because frogs live on land and in water and are considered *sentinel* species. A sentinel is one who guards or watches. It's possible that anything that affects frogs could one day affect *us*. That's why we should care."

The last speaker was Carlos. "We can show our concern for frogs in many ways. First of all, there's a need for education. We must learn everything we can about the subject and then help spread the message to others.

"There's at least one office that deals with environmental matters in every state. You can contact them to see what volunteer opportunities they

Make an inference: What kinds of things that affect frogs could also affect us? Do you think we should be concerned? Why or why not?

have. Your local library is a good place to find their names and addresses.

"And if you have access to a computer, the information you can get by yourself is enormous. You could start with *www.frogweb.gov* or *www.amphibiaweb.org*. You'll get more links than you can imagine. You can get maps and lists of the frog species found in your area. Please help the frogs—please do it now!"

This story is based on a real class project. In August 1995, a teacher by the name of Cindy Reinitz took her class from the New Country School in Henderson County, MN, on a field trip. They made the discovery described in this story. In addition, they spread the word that brought the frog problem into the spotlight. Representatives from all types of media interviewed the students. The frog project that Ms. Reinitz' students developed earned them first prize in a competition entitled "A Pledge and a Promise Environmental Awards." ●

Looking at Both Sides

In the article, the students gave possible reasons why some frogs are deformed. This information is presented from the perspective of the students. Choose one reason—such as the use of chemical pesticides. Think of a person or group of people who might have a different perspective on the matter and explain what their viewpoint might be.

The Environment Matters

What environmental issue matters most to you—recycling, conserving forests, protecting endangered animals, or something else? Write a paragraph explaining your feelings about one issue. Describe something you can do personally to address the matter.

Funny Stuff

Write one or two of your own jokes or riddles about frogs, salamanders, or another amphibian. Add illustrations, too.

FOOD IN THE BALANCE

Do you eat a balanced diet? For one day, record everything you eat. Figure out the number of servings you eat of each group on the Food Pyramid by using the chart at right. For example, a sandwich counts as two servings of bread. If you eat something that combines food groups, be sure to count everything. A slice of pepperoni pizza fits into the cheese, bread, and meat groups!

JUST HOW MUCH IS "ONE SERVING"? HERE ARE SOME HINTS:

Beans	1/2 cup cooked
Bread	1 slice
Cereal	1 ounce (1/2 to 3/4 cup)
Cheese	one-inch cube
Eggs	1
Fruit juice	3/4 cup
Fruit	1 medium piece
Meat or Fish	2–3 ounces (the size of a deck of cards)
Milk or Yogurt	1 cup
Peanut butter	2 tablespoons
Vegetables	1/2 cup cooked or 1 cup raw

DOUBLE CHECK

When is a serving not a serving? When it's more or less than one! Check out the labels on food packages. What is considered one serving?

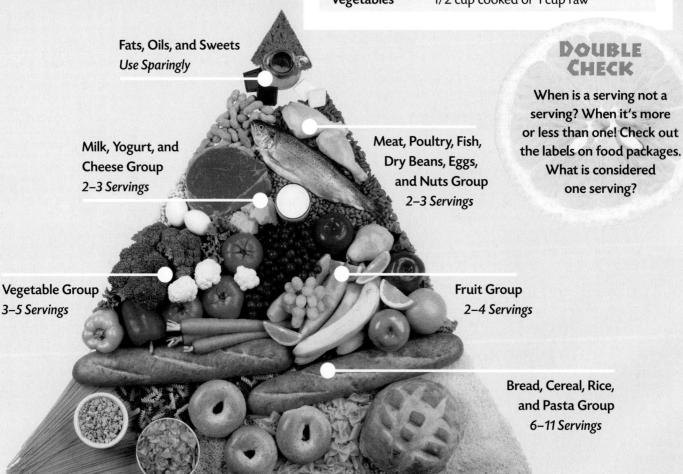

Fats, Oils, and Sweets
Use Sparingly

Milk, Yogurt, and Cheese Group
2–3 Servings

Meat, Poultry, Fish, Dry Beans, Eggs, and Nuts Group
2–3 Servings

Vegetable Group
3–5 Servings

Fruit Group
2–4 Servings

Bread, Cereal, Rice, and Pasta Group
6–11 Servings

The United States Department of Agriculture suggests using this Food Pyramid as a guide to healthy eating.

A BALANCING Act

by Brad Herzog

What do a free throw and a cartwheel have in common? How about the ski slopes and the tennis courts? Or a home run swing and a hole-in-one? The answer is: balance.

In some sports, it helps to be strong or quick or flexible or fearless. But nearly every sport requires some kind of balance, whether you're diving into a pool, skating on ice, or aiming for the green on a golf course. Just ask the kids who compete.

DANIELLE

Danielle

Eleven-year-old Danielle Reeder has been figure skating in Northbrook, Illinois, since she was six years old. She knows how important balance is while skating, but Danielle has also discovered that it plays a part in other activities she enjoys, like hip-hop dancing, ice dancing, and volleyball. She takes tennis lessons, too, and there again, balance is the key.

Why do you think balance is important in these activities?

"You have to make sure you have the right balance or the ball will go where you *don't* want it to go," says Danielle. In fact, a proper tennis swing requires balancing your feet with your arm swing. "You step into it and swing," says Danielle. "To make it full, you have to bring the racket up and follow through. If you're not balanced, the ball might go out or over the line."

Will

Will Frizzell is an eleven-year-old athlete in Boise, Idaho. He has been skiing since he was eight years old, and he believes balance is the most important part of shushing down the slopes. "When you want to turn, you have to lean a certain way, and you need good balance," he says. "If your body is turned sideways too much or you lean too far, you'll fall over."

Of course, skiing isn't only about moving left and right. After all, the point is to go down the hill. In fact, skiers must strike a careful balance between moving forward and leaning backward. "You have to keep a lot of weight on the back of your boots, so you won't go flying forward," Will explains. And what happens if you lean too far forward? What else? "You'll fall over," says Will.

Besides strutting his stuff on the slopes, Will likes to spend time in the swimming pool. He competes in swim meets in three different strokes—freestyle, butterfly, and backstroke. In the backstroke, swimmers start in the water. But in the freestyle and butterfly, they start by diving from the side of the pool. Guess what that requires? That's right. Balance.

"Your feet have to be in a certain position, and you throw yourself forward," says Will. "It's important to keep your weight balanced on the back of your feet when you push off." Much like skiing, the position requires a balance between leaning forward and backward. You want to be leaning toward the water and ready to dive in as soon as possible, but you don't want to lean too far, or you'll fall in.

Eleanor

Like Will, twelve-year-old Eleanor Steven also lives in Boise, and has been competing in sports for many years. Eleanor began tumbling and doing cartwheels when she was three, and was a gymnast for six years. Balance is a key skill for every gymnastics event, including the vault, floor exercise, and the uneven bars.

But there is one event in which balance is everything—the balance beam, of course! The balance beam is 4 feet off the ground and only 4 inches wide. Still, gymnasts do flips and back handsprings on it! It takes incredible balance and amazing concentration.

"During a cartwheel or a backward walkover, you have to have your body lined up with the beam," says Eleanor. "If you're straight, you'll always catch the beam."

Eleanor stopped competing in gymnastics when she was nine. Instead, she took up a different sport. Eleanor had taken ballet lessons when she was very little, and she liked to dance. She also enjoyed the athletic skills involved with gymnastics. So Eleanor picked a sport that was a balance between the two—part dance and part sports. She became a figure skater.

"One of the first things you learn is balancing on one leg for as long as you can," says Eleanor. "Once you get used to it, then you try to spin." Skaters are supposed to spin on the inside edge of their blade, which requires another kind of balance. "The blade on your skate has an inside edge and an outside

edge," she says. "You have to balance yourself on one or the other, whichever one you're meant to be on."

Where you balance on your blade is also an important part of a tricky element in figure skating—jumps. In fact, any jump on the ice requires a combination of balancing skills. You have to balance on one leg as you ease into the jump, balance on the correct part of the blade when you take off, and then maintain your balance when you land. That's quite a balancing act!

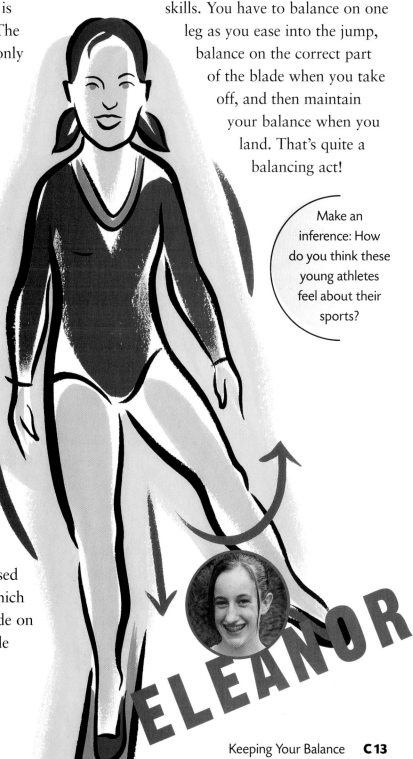

Make an inference: How do you think these young athletes feel about their sports?

ELEANOR

CORINNA

Corinna

Eleven-year-old Corinna Rees lives in Pebble Beach, California, which is famous for its world-class golf courses. She knows that a successful golf swing "hangs in the balance." Corinna has been perfecting her golf swing since she was two years old. In fact, when she was ten she produced a swing that must have been nearly perfect. Her ball flew over a river, bounced onto the green, and rolled straight into the cup—a hole-in-one!

Corinna has been taught how to swing a golf club properly. "You have to rotate around your spine, and your feet have to be sturdy," she explains. "You can't rock on your feet because you lose your balance that way."

Corinna also knows that golf isn't only about balancing your feet. It's about balancing your body with your golf club and with the ground. Golfers don't always have a flat surface to hit from. They can be facing uphill, downhill, or even the side of a hill.

And then there's one more thing they have to balance—their emotions. "When your shot is over, there's nothing you can do to change it, so why get mad? You can't get too happy either, because then you generally hit bad shots," says Corinna. "I was pretty excited playing the hole after my hole-in-one, and I think I got an eight. It was pretty bad."

Why is it important to keep your emotions in balance? How would feeling too happy or too mad affect your performance?

James

Of course, baseball is another sport where the swing is the thing. "While batting, you start off with your weight back, then take a stride and put your weight forward. Balancing your weight is probably the most important thing," says James Laughlin, who plays center field in Pacific Grove, California.

James is also a very good basketball player. In fact, he won a county free-throw shooting championship. Naturally, balance is important at the free-throw line, too. "I try to keep my body straight. Don't lean back or forward," he says. "Lean too far forward, and you tend to shoot it too hard. It doesn't go in the arc you want it to. Lean too far back, and you don't get enough power behind the shot. You usually come up short."

James has found that much the same thing happens in another sport he plays—soccer. When kicking a soccer ball, if his balance is off, so is his shot. If he leans too far forward, he might kick just the top of the ball. If he's too far back, he might kick it too high in the air. Either way, it won't go very far.

Clearly, balance is a necessary part of nearly any physical activity—from diving and kicking to swinging and spinning. But kids like Danielle, Will, Eleanor, Corinna, and James compete in several sports, and that also requires them to balance their time between the games they play and the rest of their lives.

"Family first, school second, and sports third," says James. "That's how it should be, and that's how it is." And that may be the most important balancing act of all! ◉

Stop and Respond

Acrostic Poem

Write the word *BALANCE* down the left-hand side of a sheet of paper, one letter on each line. Then write an acrostic poem about one sport or activity that requires balance. Each line of the poem should begin with the next letter in the word. Add a title that describes or names the sport.

A High Dive

B ody straight and
A rms over my head. I
L ean forward
A nd throw myself into
N othingness. The wind
C atches at me as I tumble
E nd over end into water.

Thinking Beyond the Text

Think about the athletes who were featured in the article. Using the information about them, make an inference: What are one or two conclusions you can draw about how a young person becomes a winning competitor in a sport? Discuss with a partner.

Interview Yourself

Include yourself as another example of a young person who participates in activities that require balance. Write one or two paragraphs about a sport or activity you enjoy. Explain at least one thing you have done to become better at the sport or activity.

Getting an Earful About Balance

Riding a bicycle . . .
Walking . . .
Playing ball . . .

You may not realize it, but your ears help you do all these things. How? By helping you keep your balance.

In the inner ear are three semicircular canals. The canals look a little like a pretzel and are filled with fluid. When you move your head in any direction, the fluid in one or more of the canals moves, too. This sends signals to the brain. Then the brain passes the message along to your muscles, so the rest of your body knows what to do to keep you balanced and on your feet.

Most of the time, you don't have to think about keeping your balance. Your body adjusts itself automatically. In fact, one of the wonderful things about the inner ear is that it acts as an early-warning system. If you are about to lose your balance, your ear tells your brain to send an alert to your muscles. They do what they have to do to keep you from falling—most of the time!

Your eyes count, too!

Try this!
Stand by the kitchen counter or table. Hold your hands out flat over the counter or table, but not touching it. Balance on one foot. Now close your eyes and do the same thing. What do you discover?

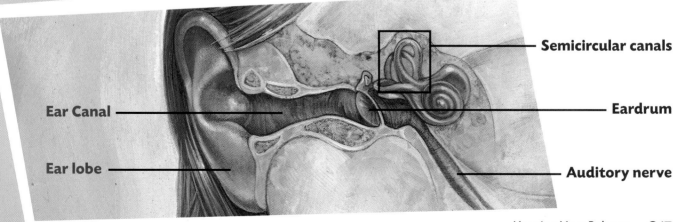

Ear Canal

Ear lobe

Semicircular canals

Eardrum

Auditory nerve

INFERRING

Poetic Defense

This morning Marta's teacher gave each student a poem to read. She asked them to be ready to explain to the class what the message of each poem is.

As Marta reads her poem, she **infers** from the text. She combines her own knowledge with the words of the poem. She forms a personal interpretation of the poem and its meaning.

> When we recycle, we tie up the newspapers and wash out containers.

> The poem says that everything goes into bins. I know that's true.

Folks Like Me

I tie up the weekly news,
I wash out jugs and tins.
I put it all at the curb
In just the proper bins.

A rain forest seedling grows;
An ocean fish glides free.
Both a little safer now—
Because of folks like me.

> I learned in science that the more people recycle, the better the environment will be.

> This poem says recycling helps save plants and animals.

Marta can defend her interpretation by pointing out what she already knows. She has background knowledge about how her family recycles and about the importance of recycling to the environment. She is also able to point to parts of the poem that support her interpretation.

Readers make connections between what they read and what they already know. They use these connections to help them interpret, understand, and remember what they read.

LIKE CLOCK-WORK

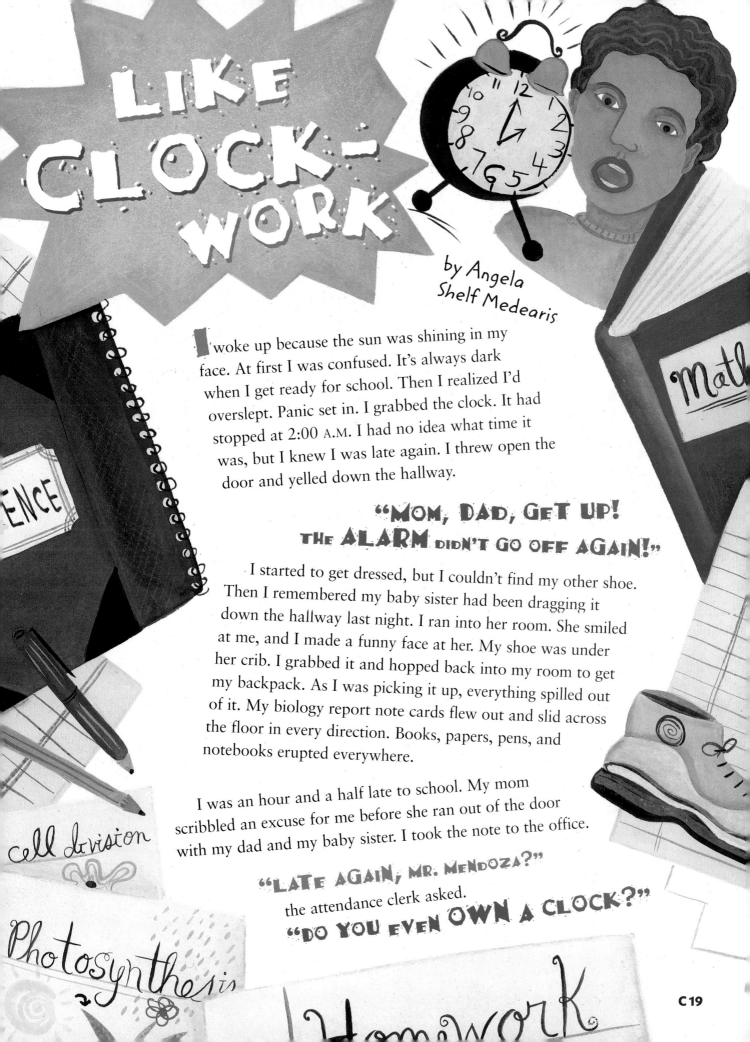

by Angela Shelf Medearis

I woke up because the sun was shining in my face. At first I was confused. It's always dark when I get ready for school. Then I realized I'd overslept. Panic set in. I grabbed the clock. It had stopped at 2:00 A.M. I had no idea what time it was, but I knew I was late again. I threw open the door and yelled down the hallway.

"MOM, DAD, GET UP! THE ALARM DIDN'T GO OFF AGAIN!"

I started to get dressed, but I couldn't find my other shoe. Then I remembered my baby sister had been dragging it down the hallway last night. I ran into her room. She smiled at me, and I made a funny face at her. My shoe was under her crib. I grabbed it and hopped back into my room to get my backpack. As I was picking it up, everything spilled out of it. My biology report note cards flew out and slid across the floor in every direction. Books, papers, pens, and notebooks erupted everywhere.

I was an hour and a half late to school. My mom scribbled an excuse for me before she ran out of the door with my dad and my baby sister. I took the note to the office.

"LATE AGAIN, MR. MENDOZA?"
the attendance clerk asked.
"DO YOU EVEN OWN A CLOCK?"

C 19

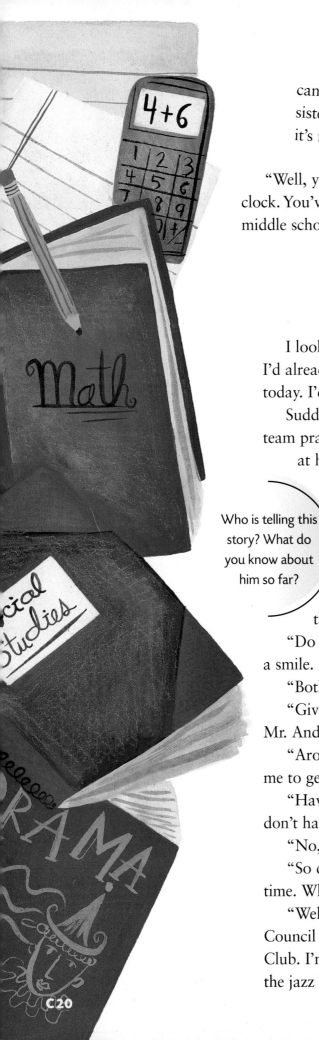

"Yes," I answered, "but I guess it's broken. Looks like you can't trust modern technology after all. And because my baby sister keeps my parents up all night, they always oversleep, so it's my job to get everyone up in the morning."

"Well, you're not doing so well as a *human* alarm clock. You've been late several times since you started middle school," the clerk said.

"YOU CAN EXPLAIN YOUR TARDY BEHAVIOR TO MR. ANDREWS, THE ASSISTANT PRINCIPAL."

I looked up at the clock as I walked to Mr. Andrews' office. I'd already missed science. My insect cataloging project was due today. I'd also missed half of social studies.

Suddenly, I remembered that I had band today and swim team practice after school. I'd left my saxophone and swimsuit at home. I'd have to call my mom and have her bring everything to school. This was turning out to be an unbelievably bad day.

"Mr. Mendoza," Mr. Andrews said, "come on in."

Mr. Andrews swiveled around in his chair and stood up to shake my hand. I gave him the file from the attendance clerk.

Who is telling this story? What do you know about him so far?

"Do you need counseling or a new clock?" he asked with a smile.

"Both," I laughed.

"Give me an idea of what a typical week is like for you," Mr. Andrews said. "What time do you get up in the morning?"

"Around 7:00," I said. "It only takes about 30 minutes for me to get ready in the morning."

"Have you ever tried getting up a half hour earlier so you don't have to rush?" Mr. Andrews asked me.

"No, I like to sleep late," I said sheepishly.

"So do I," Mr. Andrews said. "But I find I need the extra time. What's your schedule like when you get to school?"

"Well, let's see . . . I use my homeroom time for Student Council meetings. I use my lunchtime to meet with the Drama Club. I'm helping with the school fundraiser, and I'm organizing the jazz band trip."

"That's quite a lot! What happens after school?" Mr. Andrews asked.

"On Mondays, Wednesdays, and Fridays, I have swim practice and jazz band rehearsal," I continued. "On Tuesdays, Thursdays, and Saturdays, I have soccer practice and games."

"Do you have chores to do at home, too?" Mr. Andrews asked.

"I'm supposed to clean my room, help with the dishes, and take out the trash," I said. "But most of the time, I don't get much done because I have so much homework to do."

"Are you getting your homework assignments in on time?" Mr. Andrews asked.

"Sometimes I forget to do the work that the teacher assigns," I admitted. "Or I do the work and then forget to bring it to school to turn it in."

"Okay, I've heard enough," Mr. Andrews said.

"NOW I'VE GOT AN ASSIGNMENT FOR YOU."

I groaned. Mr. Andrews laughed.

"This assignment is going to make your life easier. I promise," he said.

"OK," I said skeptically. "What do I have to do?"

"Your assignment is to organize your life so that you can balance your school work, your extracurricular activities, and your home life."

"That's it?" I asked.

"It's not going to be as easy as you think," Mr. Andrews laughed. "First, I want you to turn in an organizational plan to me by Friday. On Monday morning, I want you to start your new plan. Then let me know how things are going in a week."

"OK—I guess," I said.

"You didn't write down a word I said," Mr. Andrews pointed out. "How are you going to remember all that?"

Why do you think Mr. Andrews is asking about the boy's activities?

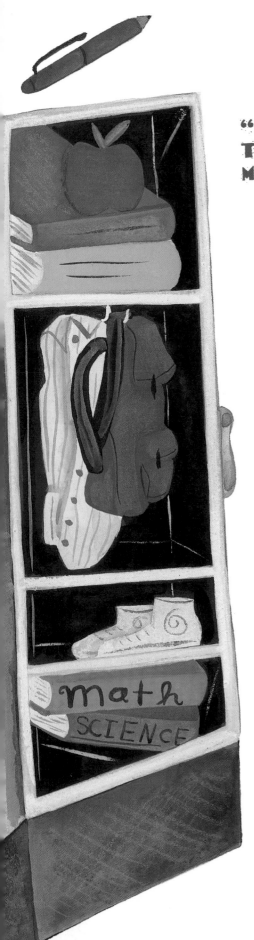

I laughed. I was beginning to get the picture. "You're right," I said.

"I GUESS THE FIRST THING I HAVE TO DO IS START WRITING DOWN MY ASSIGNMENTS."

I took out a sheet of paper. I titled the page GOALS FOR BALANCING MY LIFE and quickly listed all the things Mr. Andrews had suggested.

"Hopefully, I'll never be late again," I said.

"Well, this list is a good start," Mr. Andrews said.

The school bell rang unbearably loud. I waved good-bye to Mr. Andrews and ran to my locker to get my math book. I stared at the mess inside it and began to think about my assignment. I suppose I should start with my locker, I thought to myself. I had a few minutes to spare, so I dug right in. Actually, organizing my locker would save me time between classes. And instead of just listening when the teacher was talking, I would take notes.

So, starting with math, and for the rest of the day, I made a list of all the assignments that were due and if I had any tests coming up.

I called my mom and asked her to bring my swimsuit and saxophone to school. She was upset, but I told her that I was working on becoming more organized.

"We're *all* going to work harder on that," she said. "I just bought four of the loudest alarm clocks known to man. I'm going to set two for the time we need to get up, and two that will ring a half hour before we're supposed to leave."

"I guess I'll start getting up a half hour earlier," I said. "I'll try to use that time to do my chores and get my stuff ready for school."

"I think we all should get up earlier," Mom said. "This running around every morning is way too stressful."

At dinner that night, Dad asked, "How did your day go?"

"Pretty hectic," I said. "I've been late so many times I had to talk to the Assistant

What would you infer about this family? Do you think they will change? Why or why not?

GOALS FOR
BALANCING MY LIFE

Monday	swim practice and jazz band
Tuesday	soccer practice, homework, clean my room
Wednesday	swim practice and jazz band, homework, do the dishes
Thursday	soccer game and homework, take out the trash
Friday	swim practice and jazz band, homework
Saturday	soccer game, homework— study for math test
Sunday	family time

Principal. He wants me to come up with an organizational plan for my life."

"I have a chart at work that might help," Dad said. "Maybe I could make some copies, and we could use them as a family."

"That sounds like a great idea," I said. "Mom and I have already decided to get up earlier."

"Maybe we should use some of that time to eat breakfast together," Dad said. "Breakfast is supposed to be the most important meal of the day."

I started to feel good about the way my day had turned out. It hadn't been so unbearably bad after all.

The next day, I listed everything we'd planned to do in my report for Mr. Andrews. On Friday, when I turned it in, he smiled at me when he read how the whole family was planning on getting organized.

"Good luck," Mr. Andrews said. "See you next Friday—and hopefully it won't be because you're late again!"

"Hopefully not," I said. "See ya 'round."

On Monday, our family put our new plan into action. Mom's alarm clocks got everyone out of bed earlier. I had plenty of time to get ready for school and do my chores. Everyone knew what was scheduled for the week because we wrote it down on the chart Dad brought home from work.

Dad fixed us a great breakfast every morning. I began to enjoy getting up early so we could talk. I managed to get all my class assignments turned in on time. My grades even improved. I'm sure it's because I had notes I could look back at when I studied.

I started stopping by Mr. Andrews' office each Friday— right on time, just to check in with him.

"Well," Mr. Andrews asked. "How did everything go this week?"

"LIKE CLOCKWORK,"
I SAID, **SMILING.** ○

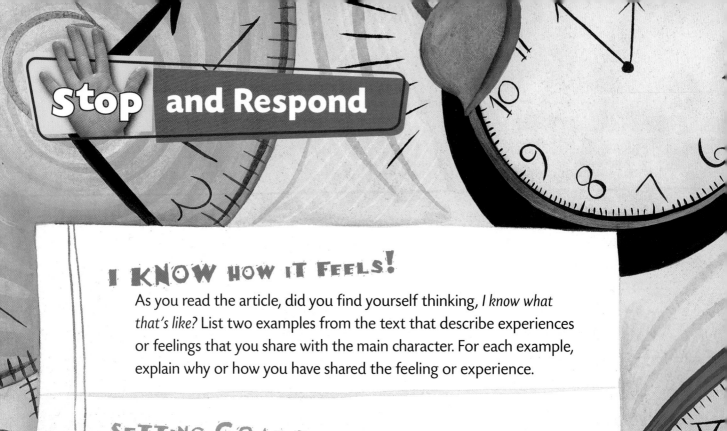

Stop and Respond

I KNOW HOW IT FEELS!

As you read the article, did you find yourself thinking, *I know what that's like?* List two examples from the text that describe experiences or feelings that you share with the main character. For each example, explain why or how you have shared the feeling or experience.

SETTING GOALS

Create your own list of GOALS FOR BALANCING MY LIFE. You can use ideas from the article and ideas of your own. Remember that the purpose of the list is to help you balance your school life, extracurricular activities, and home life.

DAILY TIME LINE

How busy are you? Make a time line for one day in your life. Start the time line with the time you get up and end it with your bedtime. Show everything you do during the day, and when you do it.

ORGANIZATIONAL POSTER

Create a poster that takes a humorous approach to helping a typical fifth-grader get organized. Be sure to illustrate your poster.

Success for Preteens

How do you succeed in fifth grade? Or in any grade for that matter? There are a few simple rules:
1. Get plenty of rest.
2. Eat healthy foods.
3. Do your homework.

But a harder question might be: How do you get plenty of rest, eat healthy foods, and do your homework in today's high-pressure, high-performance society? It's not easy.

by Denise M. Jordan

1 Get Plenty of Rest

When asked to identify the biggest problems in her life, eleven-year-old Krista said, "Getting up in the morning and keeping up with my homework." Why are these problems for Krista? Because she's tired.

Like many of today's active preteens, Krista is busy. She gets up early, washes, dresses, then fixes her hair. She eats a quick breakfast. She arrives at her elementary school early to serve as a junior crossing guard. She stays after school several days a week for cheerleading practice. Monday evenings she has dance class.

It's recommended that preteens get nine or more hours of sleep each night. That doesn't always happen, though. As a result, fatigue and lack of sleep are two of the most common complaints of today's young people. Combine an active lifestyle with the energy drain that accompanies a rapidly growing and changing body, and you can see why Krista is tired. The problem continues as preteens move into middle school.

> Make an inference: Why don't young people get the sleep and rest they need?

Asha, thirteen years old, knows all about it. Her day starts early, too. She catches the bus or gets dropped off at school by her parents. Either way, she has to get up very early to be ready on time.

Getting up early is not always easy for this student athlete. Asha plays basketball for her middle school and for another community team. When she gets home from practice, she has homework to do. It's usually close to 11:00 before Asha gets to bed. When she wakes up in the morning, she's tired.

Eat Healthy Foods

To fight the fatigue issue, Asha tries to eat a healthy diet. "I don't eat much meat," she explained. "I try to eat mostly chicken and fish and a lot of vegetables."

Asha has the right idea. It's important to eat a diet that is low in fats, salt, and sugar. It's also important to start the day with a good breakfast. Studies show that people who eat breakfast are more productive, alert, study better, and do better at sports than people who don't.

Some students say they can't eat a lot in the morning. That's OK if you're one of them. If you choose the right foods, you can get off to a good start without feeling stuffed. Eat a bowl of cereal and some fruit, or drink a glass of fruit juice and have a slice of toast, a bagel, or a muffin. Yogurt and cheese are good milk substitutes. Breakfast is important—it's the fuel that starts your engine.

If you're unable to eat a healthy breakfast, supplement it throughout the day with nutritious high-energy snacks: fresh fruit, yogurt, peanuts, or trail mix. Avoid soda pop, potato chips, and candy. Talk to your parents about the kinds of things you'd like them to buy at the grocery store.

Do Your Homework

Ten-year-old Monica's problem is not fatigue or eating right. This fifth-grade student has difficulty reading and spelling. But Monica is attacking her problem positively. Rather than complaining or giving up, Monica sees a tutor several times a week. She uses her after-school time to work on her problem areas.

If school is a struggle for you, too, ask for help. Ask your teacher, your parents, or older siblings. You can also contact your local library to find out if there is a "homework" or "study connection" in your area.

Jason, thirteen, offers this advice to students who want to do well: "Don't clown around in school." He recommends giving yourself some time to relax *after* school.

Jason likes to go online or watch television when he first gets home. He does his homework after dinner, or meets friends at the library to study in a group. However, he makes sure the study session does not turn into a gab session.

You need to find a quiet place, too. It's been proven that students don't do well studying in front of the television or with music blaring. Both are distractions—they take your mind off the lesson at hand.

It's not unusual for students to study in the kitchen. There's plenty of table space and it's usually well lit. However, if the kitchen in your house is noisy, find another spot.

Your bedroom might be a good alternative. If you share your room with a sibling, plan a time that your room can be used strictly for studying. That way, everyone is quiet and studying at the same time.

Why do you think the best time to study varies for each person?

The best time to study varies for each person. Tiffany, a sixth-grade student, says, "I like to be with my friends when I first get home from school." She spends about an hour outside with them. Then she goes inside to do her homework.

Asha offers this advice: "Keep a schedule. It helps to be organized." Write all of your activities and homework assignments in a notebook or calendar. Check it frequently. Mark off assignments or activities as you complete them.

Keeping a Balance on Stress

Too much stress can lead to poor mental and physical health, even in preteens. It's important to keep a healthy balance. Don't take on too much; learn to say no. If you're feeling stressed out and pulled in a thousand different directions, you might be doing too much. It's time to pull back and decide what you really want and need to do.

Keeping a journal or diary is one way to do this. Jot down the events of the day and describe how you felt. Make a list of the things that are important to you. Also reflect on what you are really good at, the things that you like about yourself, or the things you do well. You'll be amazed at how much better you feel about yourself after writing this kind of dialogue.

To be a successful and well-rounded person, you have to juggle a lot. Take a closer look at everything that you're doing and decide if each activity is something you really enjoy. If it's not, eliminate it. Homework doesn't count, though—your teachers and parents probably wouldn't let you give *that* up!

Try to get between nine and eleven hours of sleep each night. Eat a healthy diet. If you need help with your schoolwork, ask for it. Ask again if you don't get what you need the first time. Limit the time you spend with activities and people that keep you from achieving your goals. Remember, it's *your* life. Many things are out of your control, but if you try, you can begin to take charge of the things that *are* in your control. And then success will surely follow. ◯

Summarize the ideas in this article for successfully balancing a busy life. Which could *you* use?

DIARY

Looking for a Message

Look back at the article. Make an inference. From what the author says, what do you think her advice would be if she were talking to you? List two or three tips you think she might make about how you can be a successful preteen.

Journal Jottings

The author suggests keeping a journal or diary to reflect and reduce stress. Give it a try. Write one or two paragraphs about your day so far. You can tell what you have done, how you feel, what concerns you have—or anything else you want to write. And it's up to you whether you share this writing.

Give It Up!

If you are a student involved in several activities, imagine that you have to give up one regular activity. What would you choose and why? (Remember—you can't give up school or homework!)

Changes

This is a time of life when you are going through many changes. Write a poem or song lyrics that describe some of the changes you look forward to—or changes you wish wouldn't happen.

Let's Write

Nature in Balance

Create a rhymed or unrhymed poem about the balance of nature.
You can write about endangered animals, the environment, or
another natural theme that interests you.

Out of Balance

Imagine that you lose your sense of balance completely. Write a short
story about what happens and how you manage to get things done.

Advice for a Balanced Life

Many people talk and write about the importance of a "balanced
life." What is your definition of a balanced life for someone your age?
What advice would you give other kids to help them achieve a
balanced life?

Invention Corner

Sports equipment is always changing. New kinds of skis help skiers
turn more easily. New types of sneakers let basketball players jump
higher. Think of an invention that might help an athlete balance
better. Your idea can be something practical—or something wild and
crazy. Draw a picture of your invention and explain how it works.

More Books

Feldman, Jane. *I Am A Gymnast*. Random House, 2000.

George, Jean Craighead. *The Missing Gator of Gumbo Limbo*. HarperTrophy, 1993.

Lund, Bill. *Rock Climbing*. Capstone Press, 1996.

Moser, Adolf J. *Don't Pop Your Cork on Mondays: The Children's Anti-Stress Book*. Landmark, 1988.

Ngo, Vinh-Hoi. *The Martial Arts Almanac*. Lowell House, 1997.

Pratt, Kristin Joy. *A Walk in the Rainforest*. Dawn, 1992.

Schomp, Virginia. *If You Were . . . a Ballet Dancer*. Benchmark, 1997.

On the Web

American Ballet Theater
http://www.abt.org

The Beginner's Guide to Martial Arts
http://www.martialresource.com

Bodies in Motion . . . Minds at Rest
http://library.thinkquest.org/12153/

The Five-a-Day Challenge
http://www.dole5aday.com/menu/kids/
menu.htm

Across the Curriculum

Research

Find out about a career that requires a good sense of balance. Examples include ballet dancer, ice skater, high-wire artist, or martial arts instructor. Create a poster to share what you learn.

Science

Get some hands-on practice with balance. Construct a mobile from sticks cut to various lengths. Choose a theme for your mobile. Find or make objects that reflect the theme. Attach string to each object. Then arrange and tie the objects to the sticks so they balance.

Just Ask IGGY

Do you need help keeping things in balance? These kids certainly do! Fortunately, they have Iggy—and he's always ready with advice.

A Note from Me :-)

Dear Iggy,
I'm desperate! I have a big report due on Monday. I've been so busy I haven't even started yet! What should I do???

Desperate—Really Desperate!

Dear Really,
I have three pieces of advice for you:
1. Sharpen your pencil.
2. Go to the library.
3. Get to work!

Good luck!
Iggy

Dear Iggy,

Help! This week alone I have homework every night, band practice on Monday, a tuba lesson on Tuesday, baseball practice on Wednesday and Sunday, and games on Thursday and Saturday. Now Mom says I have to watch my kid sister on Friday night. It's not fair! What can I do?

Worn Out

Dear Worn,
Whew! Here's what I suggest. Make a list of everything you have to do and show it to your mother. Maybe she'll feel sorry for you and let you off the hook. Or maybe she'll make you give up baseball. That's the chance you take...

Yours,
Iggy

Dear Iggy,
You probably can't solve this problem, but I'm writing anyway. I want to learn how to ride a unicycle. I've been trying, but it seems hopeless. So far I have skinned both knees, sprained my thumb, and ripped my best T-shirt. What do you suggest?

Clumsy

Dear Clumsy,
Maybe trade the unicycle in for a bicycle. You'll have more fun and fewer injuries. But if you're determined to keep trying, remember balance is the key.

Your pal,
Iggy

What would *you* say?
What advice would you give to these kids? Choose one letter and write a response.

COMPREHENSION QUARTERLY

CQ

5

ISSUE D: Using and
Extending Knowledge

LIFE IN A CROWDED PLACE

Life in a Crowded Place

THINK ABOUT: Using and Extending Knowledge

D4

FICTION
On the Edge of Raining Rocks
Follow two young squirrels on their great egg hunt.

D11

NONFICTION
Caught in the Crunch
Find out about some jam-packed places in the animal kingdom.

D19

FICTION
Suite Julia
All Julia wants is a little peace and quiet. Can she get it?

D25

NONFICTION
Packed Places
Recipe for a crowd: Bring too many people together.

USING AND EXTENDING KNOWLEDGE

Let's Go!

"It's awesome! We get to plan the trip ourselves, and we'll be gone the whole day!" Jorge was talking to his best friend, Ben, about Mr. Steinbeck's fifth-grade class's field trip to the city.

Over the next several weeks, the class worked together to plan the trip. The students used what they already knew from their personal experiences in the city as well as what they read in guide books, brochures, and other materials for tourists.

In reading guide books, students found out that the children's museum was closed on the day they were going. Since many students had enjoyed reading *Island of the Blue Dolphins,* Jorge shared some materials from the aquarium. Included in this was a schedule that showed a daily dolphin show. Meanwhile, Jolina showed the class a brochure about the science museum's big-screen theater. The featured movie was about theme park rides. Since the class was studying forms of energy in science, Mr. Steinbeck and the students decided that the roller coaster movie would be a fun way to learn about force and motion. With Mr. Steinbeck's assistance, Jorge and Jolina reserved seats for the two shows.

The class, together with the bus driver, Ms. Tresnowski, then figured out the best route to get the group around the crowded city quickly. They looked at street maps and even called a TV station's traffic reporter for advice. By using multiple sources, they planned departure times from school and the museums.

When the plans for the field trip were set, Mr. Steinbeck encouraged the students to read about dolphins and the different kinds of theme park rides. He explained that the more students **used and extended** their background **knowledge** about the topics, the more they would benefit from the field trip.

Think about a time when you planned a trip. How did you use something that you already knew to help you? What kinds of things did you read to gather more information about the trip?

Schedule:

10:30 AM   Science museum: big screen movie about theme park rides

2:00 PM   Aquarium: Dolphin show

On the Edge of Raining Rocks

by Brad Herzog

There once was a tree on a hill. It used to be one of many trees on the hill. In the many trees lived many animals. Birds bounced from branch to branch. Chipmunks chased each other. Squirrels scampered. Caterpillars crawled. And ants argued.

"That's my bread crumb!"

"No, that's mine!"

You've never heard an ant argue? Well, you just haven't listened closely enough.

All of the animals got along rather well. It was a family in a forest. But then the golf course arrived, and the forest became a fairway. The trees were chopped down one by one, and as the trees disappeared, so did most of the animals. When the chopping was finally over, only one tree was left standing—one very crowded tree.

A colony of ants lived at the bottom of the Great Tree, not far from a group of chipmunks. Some caterpillars took over one branch as they prepared to blossom into butterflies.

In a big hole in the middle of the tree lived a family of squirrels. There was a roof over the entrance to the hole. It was a folded golf

scorecard. Of course, the squirrels didn't know what golf was. After all, have you ever seen a squirrel swing a club?

At the very top of the tree lived Mr. and Mrs. Bird. Their nest was made of sticks and twigs and broken golf tees. Of course, they didn't know that, either. Have you ever seen a bird make a birdie?

One day, as two young squirrels were busy collecting acorns that had fallen from the tree, they heard a loud voice from far above. "Sammy! Sally!" It was Mrs. Bird. There was no mistaking that voice. Often, when she tried to shout, it came out sounding like a shrill scream.

Sammy and Sally Squirrel climbed to the top of the tree with such speed that they startled Mrs. Bird. "Children!" she scolded. "I like to be surprised once in a while, but I don't enjoy being shocked!"

Then she began a speech. Actually, it was more of a lecture. "You're growing up," she began. "It's time you learned responsibility . . . ."

As she continued to talk, the squirrels grew nervous. Had they done something wrong?

Were they in some sort of trouble? They didn't like trouble, especially trouble with Mrs. Bird.

Finally, Mrs. Bird came to the point. She pointed to an egg sitting in the nest. The squirrels knew it was about to hatch. Everyone knew that. It was the talk of the tree. "Mr. Bird and I have to search for food before our egg hatches," she chirped. "We'd like you to watch over it while we're gone."

The squirrels nearly jumped off the branch with joy. This wasn't trouble at all. Maybe a challenge, but not trouble. Or so they thought . . .

"Now, be careful," said Mrs. Bird. And as she flew away, she looked back at the squirrels. It wasn't a curious look in her eyes. It was a concerned look.

Sammy and Sally began by standing guard over the egg. Then they got a little tired and sat down. Soon they were bored. Finally, the two young squirrels grew downright restless.

When have you felt bored? What did you do? What do you predict Sammy and Sally will do?

"I'm going to take a closer look at this egg," said Sally, and with that she picked up the round white egg and began to examine it.

"I want to see it, too," Sammy protested and tried to grab it.

As the squirrels argued, the egg wobbled. Then it teetered. Finally, it popped into the air and over the side of the nest. The squirrels froze with fear as the egg rolled left and right, moving from one branch to another, down toward the bottom of the tree.

When the egg landed with a soft thud in a pile of leaves and began to rumble down the hill, the squirrels gasped with fright. When it scooted across a golf cart path, rolled through a sand trap, and bounced off a rubbery plant and over a small creek, the squirrels squealed with horror.

Then they saw where the egg was headed. That's when they panicked.

> What have you chased after? How does this help you understand what's happening?

"Oh no!" groaned Sammy.

"Not there!" cried Sally.

The egg had made its way to a place every young squirrel was taught never to explore. They called it Raining Rocks.

Of course, the squirrels had no way of knowing that Raining Rocks was actually a driving range, a place where golfers practiced their swings. To the squirrels, the golf balls that landed in the field every few seconds were big, white boulders raining down on them.

In the old days, before the trees were cut down to make room for humans and golf holes, Raining Rocks was known to the squirrels as Pleasant Meadow. Young squirrels used to play there all the time. It wasn't dangerous at all. But not anymore.

Sally sighed. Sammy gulped. They had to get the egg back, and they had to do it quickly. So the adventurous squirrels set out for Raining Rocks.

They rushed from branch to branch, making their way to the bottom of the Great Tree. They thumped into the pile of leaves, rushed down the hill, and headed for the golf cart path.

The squirrels had never heard of golf carts. To them, the path was an enormous road. Big Tank Road, they called it. After all, to a squirrel a simple golf cart seemed like a huge, scary tank.

In fact, just as Sammy and Sally reached the road, one of those big tanks came roaring by. The humming motor sounded like a screaming siren to the squirrels. The rumbling wheels made a thunderous sound. The rattling golf clubs clanked. The squirrels were terrified. But Sammy and Sally darted across the road just ahead of the tank, catching their breath as it zoomed out of sight.

Next came the sand trap. But to the squirrels, it was a barren desert. In fact, that's what they called it—the Barren Desert. Sammy took a deep breath. Sally did the same. And they headed across the desert, clawing their way through the sand.

"Water!" whispered Sammy after they had reached the other side.

"Yes," Sally agreed. "I could use some water, too."

Sammy shook his head and pointed to the creek over which the egg had bounced. "No," he said. "I mean, look at the water."

It was a gentle creek, only a few feet wide. But to the squirrels, it was the Rushing River. How could they possibly cross it?

Sally scratched her head. Sammy scratched his head. Then they scratched each other's head.

"I've got it!" Sally yelled. She ran over to a fallen branch and pushed it until it straddled the creek to make a bridge. Then they tiptoed carefully over the Rushing River. Well, maybe they didn't quite tiptoe. After all, have you ever seen a squirrel's toes?

After making it across, Sammy and Sally rushed up a hill. When they reached the top, they saw a terrible sight. They had hoped to find the egg in the field just ahead of them. Instead, they saw thousands of round, white objects. This was Raining Rocks. And all the "rocks" looked like eggs!

What have you experienced in your life or read about that is similar to the situation the squirrels find themselves in?

Sammy looked at Sally. Sally looked at Sammy. They both looked at the place they had been afraid of all their young squirrel lives. "Let's go!" Sammy shouted.

They rushed into the field, darting from rock to rock. It wasn't enough to just give each object a quick look. They had to stop and examine each one if they were going to find the egg. Meanwhile, every few seconds a white boulder came crashing down nearby. Sure, they were only golf balls. But they were golf balls as large as the squirrels' heads!

After several minutes, Sammy and Sally still had not found the egg. But they wouldn't give up. They couldn't give up, even as rocks rained down around them.

Suddenly, the squirrels stopped in their tracks. They had heard something. It was a very faint sound, and it sounded like . . . pecking! Sammy and Sally turned toward the sound, and there they saw an itty-bitty beak poking out of a tiny hole in a small, white object.

What do you know about hatching eggs? If you want to find out more about how eggs hatch, what could you do?

The egg!

Faster than they had ever moved before, the squirrels snatched up the egg, ran out of Raining Rocks, rushed over Rushing River, dashed through Barren Desert, and hurried across Big Tank Road. They scampered up the branches of the Great Tree and placed the egg in Mr. and Mrs. Bird's nest just as Mr. and Mrs. Bird came home.

And that was when the egg hatched. Baby Bird poked her head out and squeezed out of the shell. "Mama!" she squeaked, as she looked at Mrs. Bird.

Mrs. Bird beamed with joy. "Thank you, Sally and Sammy," she said. "I'm sorry we're so late. It must have been a bit boring for you."

"Right," thought the squirrels. "Real boring." ○

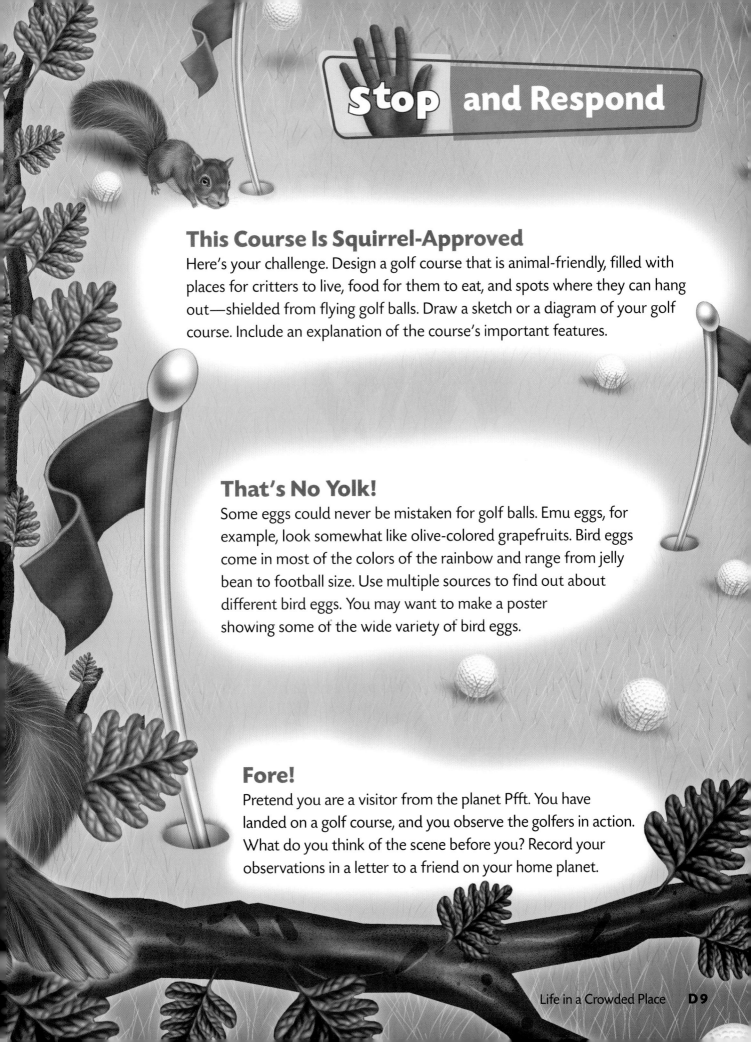

Stop and Respond

This Course Is Squirrel-Approved

Here's your challenge. Design a golf course that is animal-friendly, filled with places for critters to live, food for them to eat, and spots where they can hang out—shielded from flying golf balls. Draw a sketch or a diagram of your golf course. Include an explanation of the course's important features.

That's No Yolk!

Some eggs could never be mistaken for golf balls. Emu eggs, for example, look somewhat like olive-colored grapefruits. Bird eggs come in most of the colors of the rainbow and range from jelly bean to football size. Use multiple sources to find out about different bird eggs. You may want to make a poster showing some of the wide variety of bird eggs.

Fore!

Pretend you are a visitor from the planet Pfft. You have landed on a golf course, and you observe the golfers in action. What do you think of the scene before you? Record your observations in a letter to a friend on your home planet.

Monkey Business

With their forest homes dwindling, monkeys in many parts of Asia have moved to town. The small city of Lop Buri, Thailand, is being overrun by macaques *(ma KAKS)*, a species of long-tailed monkey.

The macaques are cute and a lot more fun to watch than the pigeons or squirrels that live in most cities. But they can be big trouble. If begging doesn't convince someone to hand over a tasty banana or orange, a forty-pound macaque might just decide to grab it and run. Sometimes bands of macaques work together. Some will distract the person with the goodies while another steals the food. These pesky monkeys have been known to snatch earrings and eyeglasses, throw things at

The macaques have taken over this table.

cars causing collisions, and climb through the windows of buildings. No wonder so many windows in Lop Buri have bars!

So why do the people of Lop Buri put up with these monkey pests? One reason comes from the culture's religious traditions. The people believe in the sacredness of all life, so they are very good-humored and understanding about the macaques. Another reason why the people of Lop Buri don't want to ship the macaques out of town is because they are the town's main tourist attraction and are good for business. The owner of one local inn even throws a big banquet for the macaques every year to thank them for helping make his business a success.

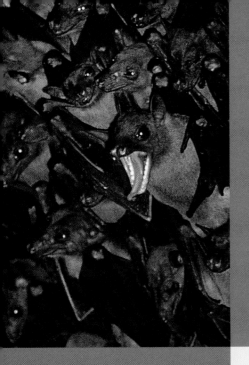

CAUGHT
IN THE
CRUNCH

by Diane Bair and Pamela Wright

Can you imagine sharing your bedroom with 10,000 others? What would you think about living in a home with more than one million inhabitants? What if you went to dinner and there were thousands sitting at the table?

There are lots of jam-packed places in the animal kingdom. Many creatures live among crowds their entire lives. Other animals migrate to special areas in the country, assembling in large droves to feed or nest. Often, people come from around the world to witness these spectacular animal gatherings. Sometimes animal gatherings draw people crowds, too!

Let's take a peek at three places where crowds of animals congregate. We'll travel to Nebraska to see the magnificent sandhill crane migration. We'll explore the busy and packed world of an eastern shoreline tidepool. In Texas, we'll watch as thousands of bats come out to eat. Imagine what life is like among these animal crowds.

We're hiding in an underground bunker overlooking Nebraska's Platte River. The bunker is covered in dirt and grass, except for a small row of narrow windows protruding just above the ground. Peeking through the windows, we get a glimpse of the river and surrounding meadows. It's dusk and the sun's final rays tinge the sky with vivid red hues. We're waiting for the cranes to return to the river.

We hear them coming first. The noise of flapping wings grows nearer and nearer. As we peek out the window, the sky darkens as if an enormous thundercloud has suddenly blocked the sun. It is a cloud—a huge, black cloud of sandhill cranes! Tens of thousands fill the air. "I didn't think there were this many birds in the whole world!" a young boy whispers.

We watch as waves and waves of boisterous birds descend on the river. The cranes fall out of the sky, landing like paratroopers on the river. They drop their legs, setting their wings as they land softly in the water, feet first. We can no longer see the water; it is covered by a mass of long-legged cranes.

The spring migration of nearly 500,000 sandhill cranes to the Platte River Valley is the largest gathering of cranes in the world. Most of the cranes spend the winter season in the south, spread throughout New Mexico, Texas, and Mexico. By mid-February, they begin their migration north to their breeding grounds, ranging from Canada to Alaska and sometimes as far as Siberia.

On the way, they stop over at the Platte River, where they spend three to four weeks fattening up and storing enough energy to complete their journey. During the day, the cranes spread out to eat corn in the fields. Each evening, they return to the safe, shallow river to roost. Sometimes, 10,000 to 15,000 cranes cram into a half-mile space on the river.

The next day, we return to the Platte River at sunrise. Big flakes of wet snow and a cold breeze hit our faces as we stand on the viewing platform. Every now and then, a lone crane rises from the darkness, a black silhouette against a murky sky. And then another flies, and another. Then, the rest of the gigantic flock rises at once, and we watch splendid waves of birds filling the sky.

What do you already know about migration?

SANDHILL CRANES

TIDEPOOLS

The air is rich with the smell of the sea. We trudge along the rocky shoreline with plastic containers and magnifying glasses in hand. It's low tide, so the beach is a wide expanse of sand and exposed, slippery rock. We come to a tidepool, a pocket of ocean water left between two rocks when the tide went out. When we first peer into the puddle, we don't see much. But when we look more closely, things begin to appear. It's a living, moving collage of sea creatures!

Lots of worms are buried in the sand and hiding beneath the rocks. Some are brown or gray. One is pink!

We notice brown rockweed, Irish moss, and a bright green sea lettuce. Snails are clinging to rocks, and clams nestle in the sand.

We find a limpet hugging the side of a rock. Its shell looks like an Oriental straw hat. A periwinkle has sealed itself to the rock, too, waiting for the next tide to come in. Periwinkles connect themselves to rocks with sticky mucus produced by their foot. When the tide comes back in, the periwinkle will resume crawling over rocks, eating algae.

Many mussels and barnacles are stuck on the rocks in the tidepool. When we look closely, we see a tiny, half-inch sea spider creeping over the top of one of the mussels.

There are lots of different amphipods swimming about in the water. Amphipods are the tiny, bug-like creatures that scuttle around rocks and swim on their sides. Beach fleas, skeleton shrimp, and scuds are all amphipods.

At the bottom of the tidepool, we spot a starfish and a sea urchin. We put them in a bucket of seawater to take a closer look. We use a magnifying glass to spot the tiny red dots at the end of the starfish's arms. These are its eyes. The sea urchin looks like a small ball covered with spikes. We put them back in the water.

We lift a pile of seaweed, and a brittle star moves. It looks like a sea star but with wavy, snaky arms. We spot something that looks like a flower. It's a sea anemone.

The more we look, the more we find—all living together in one small puddle of seawater!

> What else have you heard or read about animals that live along the seashore?

BATS

It seems like a funny place to go bat watching. We're in the congested, bustling city of Austin, Texas. There are crowds of people everywhere waiting to see the bats come out from under the Congress Avenue Bridge. It's twilight, the time when bats wake up and leave their roost to hunt for food.

The sky darkens and suddenly, without warning, the bats emerge from below the bridge and spiral into the air like a large plume of smoke. More than a million bats blanket the sky, fluttering their large wings in a jerky, swooping flight.

Each spring, Mexican free-tail bats leave their wintering grounds in Mexico and come to Austin for the summer. When the engineers reconstructed Austin's Congress Avenue Bridge in 1980, they had no idea that the crevices beneath the bridge would form ideal bat roosts. Although a few bats had lived there for years, the flying mammals began moving in by the hundreds of thousands. Today, a million and a half bats live in the colony. It's the largest urban bat colony in North America.

During the day, the bats, each about three inches long, squash together in the bridge's dark nooks and crannies. They hang upside down to rest and sleep. The bats are nocturnal. This means they are most active during the night when they come out to catch and eat insects.

Many bats, like the Mexican free-tails, use echolocation to find food and to avoid objects in the dark. They make sounds through their noses or mouths. When the sounds hit an object, the echoes bounce back to the bats and let them know that an object is near. They can even recognize the sizes and shapes of objects through echolocation. For example, they can sense if an insect is a mosquito or a moth.

Bats can eat amazing amounts of food for their size, as much as their entire body weight in one night! It's estimated that the Austin bats will devour an average of 10,000 to 30,000 pounds of insects every night.

As the sun rises, the bats return to the roost. Imagine the sight: a million and a half tiny creatures, with velvety fur and long tails, squished together, hanging beneath the Congress Avenue Bridge.

If you wanted to find out more about bats, what would you do?

A FULL HOUSE

- The underground nest of some ants can house up to 10 million ants. Driver ants of Africa and army ants of South America cling together in large groups of 10,000 to 500,000 as they travel across the land, looking for food and attacking animals in their way.

- Most bees are social animals. They live in large colonies (sometimes called hives) with tens of thousands of other bees. Honeybee colonies, for example, have an average of 60,000 individual bees.

- Walrus Islands State Game Sanctuary in Alaska is famous for its summer residents—8,000 to 12,000 male walrus. There are also about 600 to 1,000 sea lions and nearly 450,000 nesting seabirds.

- Hundreds of thousands of monarch butterflies winter at Natural Bridges State Beach in California, the largest butterfly wintering site in the United States.

What do you already know about some of these animals?

Stop and Respond

Once There Were Millions

Once, millions of buffalo roamed the plains and the skies were filled with passenger pigeons. Now buffalo are raised on ranches and passenger pigeons are gone forever. What other animals that were once abundant are now extinct or nearly so? Use multiple sources to find information about an extinct or endangered species. Then write a paragraph describing the animal and explaining how it became extinct or endangered.

Going Batty

Write a skit from the point of view of the sandhill cranes on the Platte River, the bats in Austin, or the residents of a tidepool. What is your crowded life like? What do you think of the many visitors who come to observe you?

Look Again

Sit quietly for a few moments and imagine a bee hive, an anthill, or some other animal-packed environment. Write about or sketch what you see in your mind's eye. Compare your writing or drawing with a classmate's.

Operation Cleanup

Ashley's bedroom was a very crowded place. Her parents had only two rules about Ashley's bedroom—no bad smells and keep the door shut. Ashley's room might have stayed jam-packed for a very long time, except for the disaster. Ashley's gerbil, Einstein, disappeared. Einstein was last seen in Ashley's bedroom, and no one was willing to plow through the mess to help her find him.

Ashley figured that as long as she had to search through everything, she might as well clean up. Her mother donated six plastic milk crates, a laundry bag, and a whole box of garbage bags. Ashley took a long, slow breath and began. Once she got a rhythm going, the cleanup went pretty quickly—garbage, storage, laundry, over and over. Along the way, Ashley made some interesting discoveries. She found last year's stash of candy from the school band candy sale. She found notes for a paper that she had finished in third grade, and most fascinating of all she found the bedroom carpet, something she hadn't seen since the first week they had moved into the house.

Ashley's room was beginning to look more livable and less crowded, but she still hadn't found Einstein. She was beginning to wonder whether she had accidentally stuffed Einstein into a garbage or laundry bag, so she listened for scratching sounds. Sure enough, she heard faint noises. And they were coming from Einstein's cage! There was Einstein, calm as could be, fluffing up his nest of cedar shavings. As she dashed over to shut the cage door, a thought crossed Ashley's mind. Was her room so crowded and messy that even a gerbil hadn't wanted to live there?

USING AND EXTENDING KNOWLEDGE

We're Back!

Mr. Steinbeck's fifth graders had a terrific field trip. Jolina thought the dolphin show was exciting. She sat right up front and got soaking wet as the dolphins dived, fetched, and jumped through hoops. She even had a chance to pet the oldest dolphin, Junie, on the head!

Jorge thought the movie about theme park rides was awesome, and some of the information he learned from it made Jorge change his mind about roller coasters. Before he saw the movie, he was certain that roller coasters were the scariest rides. Now he wasn't so sure.

The next day, Jolina went to the school resource center. She was eager to find information about becoming a dolphin trainer. The librarian helped her locate books and several magazine articles about dolphin training. She also found the address of a marine park and research center and planned to write its director for information about the kind of training and education you need to get a job as a dolphin trainer.

After returning from their museum field trip, Jorge decided to research theme parks within a day's drive of his home to find out what kinds of roller coasters they have. He discovered in a nonfiction book that the largest wooden roller coaster was located just 50 miles from his home. He also found that the roller coaster with the steepest vertical drop was at a theme park 100 miles away. He planned to use this information to convince his parents to take him on a roller coaster adventure vacation.

Theme park	Distance	Rides
Wild Rapids	100 miles	steepest
Thunder Point	50 miles	largest
Sea Breeze	80 miles	newest
Adventure Park	440 miles	oldest

Think about a place you have visited or something that you have done that made you want to learn more about it. How did you go about finding more information to **extend your knowledge** about the topic?

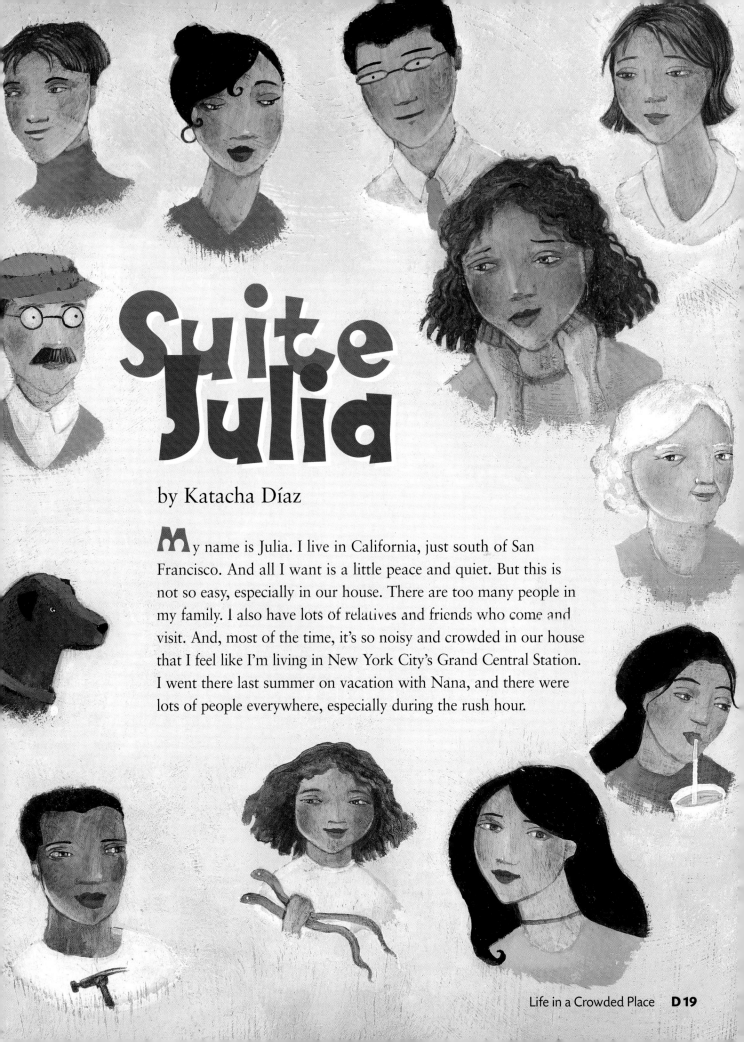

Suite Julia

by Katacha Díaz

My name is Julia. I live in California, just south of San Francisco. And all I want is a little peace and quiet. But this is not so easy, especially in our house. There are too many people in my family. I also have lots of relatives and friends who come and visit. And, most of the time, it's so noisy and crowded in our house that I feel like I'm living in New York City's Grand Central Station. I went there last summer on vacation with Nana, and there were lots of people everywhere, especially during the rush hour.

Even though I live in a crowded house, it's a lot of fun when people come and visit. When my cousin Nikki comes to spend the weekend with me, we stay up late, play computer games, and fix our favorite mango smoothies. Most of our friends and relatives come for short visits and then leave—well, with the exception of Auntie Calypso and her dog, Keeper. They came to visit for a week, and it's been over a year now—and they're still at our house!

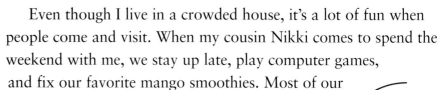

What other characters or acquaintances does Auntie Calypso remind you of? Why?

Auntie Calypso is my dad's younger sister. Mom says, "Calypso is the wanderer in our family."

Dad just chuckles and says, "That's right, dear, but you must agree that my sister has verve and lots of it." And he's right!

My Auntie Calypso is so lucky because when she wants a little peace and quiet, she goes to Cosmo's old room and hangs a "Don't Disturb" sign on the door. Cosmo is my half-brother who is away at college studying to become a doctor.

The other day when I had some time on my hands, I peeked in to see what Auntie Calypso was doing. I saw her lounging on Cosmo's bed, reading a travel magazine, and eating her favorite bittersweet bonbons! She was in her own little world and didn't even notice me.

Today when I peeked in, Auntie Calypso was sitting on the floor doing yoga exercises, and she did notice me. My aunt explained that she must stay limber and in good shape because otherwise she'll be too stiff to dance. And that would be very bad news because Auntie Calypso is passionate about Latin music and dancing—especially the tango, a popular dance in Argentina, South America.

"Can you hear the beat and feel the energy?" she asked Edgar, the postman with the moustache and beard, who came to deliver the mail yesterday. In a flash, Edgar found himself dancing the tango on our front porch.

"I'm not a good dancer," stammered Edgar.

"Don't worry," reassured Auntie Calypso, flashing Edgar her Mona Lisa smile. "You're doing just great!"

Poor Edgar! His moustache twitched a little and he stumbled a couple of times, but Auntie Calypso was determined to teach

him how to tango and kept him moving from one end of the porch to the other. But soon, and much to Edgar's relief, the dance was over.

Then there's my dad who is a rising star at one of those new dot-com companies. He has his very own office building downtown in the business district. Dad's office is big and fancy. It has comfy leather chairs and marble floors and even a small refrigerator! And I know that's where he goes when he wants some peace and quiet.

Ms. Birdsong-Bolton, his assistant, answers the phone and says, "I'm sorry, but he's in a meeting right now and cannot be interrupted. May I take a message?" I have a hunch, though, that my dad's not busy at all. He just doesn't want to be disturbed because he's having fun surfing the Web on his brand-new laptop computer. He's lucky because he gets to spend time alone there, so he has peace and quiet.

My older sister Daisy has a small room all to herself. She's lucky because most of the time she has peace and quiet. But Daisy is boy-crazy and spends all her time yakking on the phone or out on a date. Not long ago, my parents insisted she get her own phone because our family and friends complained that the line was always busy. I'm glad Daisy got her own phone because now I don't hear Mom or Dad saying, "Time to get off the phone, Daisy."

Daisy doesn't have time to notice me, except when she's going out on a date and wants me to answer her phone. Daisy smiles and says, "I'll pay you a quarter for each message you take, Julia. And how about if I give you my tropical-flavor lip gloss and let you borrow some of my glow-in-the-dark sparkles nail polish?"

And I say, "You got yourself a deal; let's shake on it!" The best part is that I get to spend time alone in Daisy's room. And, when her phone isn't ringing off the hook, I finally get a little peace and quiet.

Who does Daisy remind you of in your life? How does this help you understand the story?

Mom says that sometimes she can't even hear herself think with all the nonstop noise in our house. So when Mom wants peace and quiet she announces that she's off for some R and R. That means she's going upstairs to her bedroom for rest and relaxation. When anyone knocks on her door she asks, "Is it a life-or-death emergency? If not, please go away and let me enjoy some peace and quiet for a change."

What do you and your family members do for some R and R?

In her bedroom, Mom puts on her favorite music. Lately she's been on a Brazilian jazz kick. She even sings along in Portuguese while she takes a leisurely bubble bath. Sometimes she mashes an avocado and adds some other stuff to it and gives herself a facial.

One time she forgot to close her bedroom door and I peeked. Mom was lounging on her bed with a towel wrapped around her head, just like a turban. She also had the avocado stuff smeared all over her face and had cucumber slices over her eyelids! Yikes! I can't imagine why she does this, but she says when I grow up I'll understand why and do the same. I'm not so sure about that.

There are not enough bedrooms to go around, so I must share mine with my younger sister, Mimi. She's always running around the house shouting and making lots of noise, chasing her imaginary friends or Auntie Calypso's dog. Sometimes my mother says, "It's a beautiful day! Why don't you and Keeper go play outside?" That means she's tired of Mimi's ruckus.

Mimi is a little pest who waits for me to leave our room so she can do somersaults on my bed and hide rubber snakes under my pillows. Of course, I get angry and accidentally throw the snakes out the window! Sometimes they land on the hood of Dad's new sports car. When that happens I run downstairs and get them off the convertible before he sees them. Otherwise, I'll be in big trouble.

I had a dream the other night that my bed was up on a loft. It was my very own secret hideaway. The only way to reach my loft was to climb on a ladder. There were built-in shelves where I kept my collection of stuffed animals, the jewelry box Auntie Calypso gave me for my birthday, and my favorite books. It was also a place where my friends and I would hide out and play. "Suite Julia" was awesome, and it's just what I needed!

What did you know before you read the story that helped you better understand it?

I shared my dream with Mom and Dad and even drew a picture of it. They said "Suite Julia" was a terrific idea! Mom called Mr. Charles, our next-door neighbor, and asked him to come over and take measurements to build the loft. Mr. Charles is very clever and makes furniture at his workshop. Dad says Mr. Charles is the best carpenter in the area, and his prices are reasonable, too.

Mr. Charles did a great job building my loft and, like the one in my dreams, it's awesome! Now there's no way Mimi, the pest, can accidentally do somersaults on my bed or hide rubber snakes under my pillows, if you know what I mean.

Finally, I have a little peace and quiet. ○

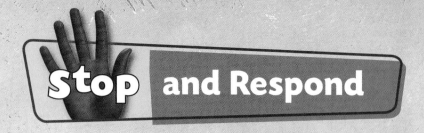

Stop and Respond

Personal Opinion

What's the most fun—being an only child or having brothers and sisters? Write your thoughts and ideas on paper. Decide on the best strategy to use in presenting your point of view. Hold an informal debate and have an audience decide which strategy made the most persuasive argument.

Plan a Place

What would you do if you had to share your bedroom with another person? Could you do it in a way that both of you still had some privacy? Think of creative ways to share your space. Sketch a plan or write a paragraph.

As stuffed as a . . .

Make a list of similes about crowds and crowded places. Here's an example: as *crowded as gumballs in a gumball machine.* After you make a list of at least eight similes, use some of them in a poem about living in a crowded place or being part of a crowd.

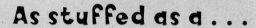

Packed Places

by Jamie Kyle McGillian

Taylor, a fifth grader from Westchester, New York, doesn't like amusement parks when they're full. He doesn't like swimming pools if they're packed with swimmers. And even though he loves baseball, he'd rather watch a game on television than sit in a baseball stadium in the company of thousands of other fans.

Taylor says, "If Yankee Stadium in the Bronx, New York, holds about 55,000 seats, just imagine if everyone there had to use the bathroom at the same time. Or, what if everyone suddenly wanted a hot dog? The crowd would go wild. People would clobber each other over a hot dog. I'd rather watch the game on TV."

But what about the excitement and the adventure of being there? Doesn't the thrill of being on the scene outweigh having to deal with the crowd? Taylor doesn't think so. "It's just a problem for me to be around so many creatures."

If you're at all like Taylor, you may have a slight case of agoraphobia. According to Lisa Tager, a social worker in Massachusetts, "Agoraphobia is a fear (phobia) of crowds. For some sufferers, the fear of not being able to escape the crowd, or get help if you needed it, can be daunting."

Some agoraphobics go out of their way to avoid crowds. "These are people who are happily using their computers to shop, who are renting videos instead of going to movie theaters, and who are avoiding crowds by going places during off hours," says Tager.

When you think about it, there are so many crowded places today—sports events, rock concerts, street fairs, beaches, airports, shopping malls, and highways. Everywhere you look, you see people. Claire, a fifth grader in Hampton, Massachusetts, explains, "When I'm in a crowd, I feel like a sardine being smashed into a sardine can. I hate sardines."

When does a crowd become too much for one person to handle? It depends on the person, but according to Lisa Tager, "Most people can meet their personal space needs if they can stretch out their arms forward and to the sides, and not be touching anyone."

Cozy in a Crowd?

Billy, a fifth grader from Miami, Florida, wonders if he'll ever feel comfortable in a crowd because of his height, or lack of it. Billy is the shortest kid in his class. Last summer, at an outdoor concert, Billy was very disappointed. "I never even saw the stage. I heard the music, but I was too short to see past the crowd. Mostly, I spent my time trying to keep my nose out of people's underarms."

Being short is a definite disadvantage when dealing with crowds. Lisa, a petite advertising assistant, rides the subway every day. She explains, "On the subway, the bigger you are, the better you'll be at making your way through the crowd. Unfortunately for me, I'm too short to reach the rail to hold my balance."

And of course, when you're really tall, being in a crowd is hardly ever threatening. Aaron, a fifth grader from Oakland, California, is over six feet. Aaron says, "When I'm in a crowd, I'm usually one of the tallest. I can always find whoever is lost. But the flip side is that I am always looking down at people."

Off to work I go!

What situations have you been in that help you understand how these people feel?

"Crowded" Expressions

It's the "crowd" that gives these phrases their meaning. How many of them do you know?

The "in" crowd – refers to the cool, hip group

The "wrong" crowd – refers to those who may not make the best role models

Two's company, three's a crowd. – two individuals who want to be together and undisturbed by a third party

Work the crowd. – to mingle through groups of people and make a strong impression on them

The crowd pleaser – the person, place, or thing that is preferred by the majority

Crowd Culture

Some people don't seem to be bothered by crowds. Some people are actually excited by them. Every year, Leni, a sixth grader from Darien, Connecticut, rings in the new year with her family by going to Times Square in New York City to watch the ball drop.

Being in Times Square, also known as "the crossroads of the world," on New Year's Eve is a free event. There are no tickets required. Access is available on a first-come, first-served basis.

The crowd is huge. Spectators must be prepared to stay in one place. They are confined to viewing areas and are not permitted to move through the Square except to exit. It's usually very cold; temperatures are often below zero. Coffee places in the surrounding area supply almost 7,000 gallons of hot coffee to the chilly crowd. Almost a million people gather! That's a lot of people, and Leni is just one of them.

What other crowds have you read or heard about?

"We wait in line for hours without bathroom breaks just to get a good spot. We're completely surrounded by strangers. Some people are tourists who speak other languages. Some people are celebrating in big ways. But most people, like us, are there to be a part of something. For one night, we're at a place where history is being made," exclaims Leni.

Lost in the Crowd

If you've ever been lost in a crowd, you might understand why some people go out of their way to avoid them. Brigit, a fifth grader from Lexington, Massachusetts, remembers an incident at the circus.

"My mom agreed to meet me right outside the bathroom, but when I got out, there were a ton of people outside, and I couldn't make my way through. I started to panic. Mom wasn't anywhere. I kept thinking I saw her and then I'd realize that it wasn't her. What I didn't know was that I went out the wrong bathroom door, so I was not even in the place where my mom was waiting. I ran into the arena to find her and I saw thousands of people. That's when I thought I'd never see her again. Finally, someone from security helped me. It was so scary."

Being part of a crowd definitely has its ups and downs. Some people find excitement in a crowd. And for most, the actual rush of being on the scene to see the band, the team, the show, or whatever it is that the crowd has gathered to see, makes up for the long lines at the bathroom and the lack of personal space.

The next time you're in a crowd, take a moment to look around at all the faces, the arms, and the legs. Listen to the sound of all the voices coming together. Then ask yourself, "Who are all these people and where do they come from?"

Have you ever felt this way? What did you do?

Have you seen my mom?

What do you know now about crowds that you didn't know before?

Claustrophobia

Is There a Phobia Phobia?

People have phobias—fears that do not make rational sense—about many things, from germs to spiders to heights. Research some common phobias and communicate your findings to your class. Include the names of the phobias in your presentation and tell what they mean.

Aerophobia

Now That Was a Crowd!

Draw a picture showing yourself in a crowd and then write a caption telling about it. Include in your caption a sentence telling what you learned about crowds from this experience.

Agoraphobia

Dear Advice Person

If you were the advice columnist at a newspaper, what advice could you offer a person who is petrified of crowds? Write a letter of advice to the agoraphobic.

City vs. Country

What are some of the advantages of living in a crowded place? What are the disadvantages? Write an expository paragraph about life in a crowded place.

Superstar

Some people cause crowds to gather wherever they go. What would this experience be like? Pretend you are a famous person—a rock star, a sports star, even President of the United States. Write a journal entry that describes your feelings about being famous, causing crowds, and losing privacy.

Multitudes of Animals

Many animals, from monarch butterflies to elephant seals, gather in huge groups at some time in their lives to eat, rest, or migrate. Research an animal crowd and write a short report that describes the animal crowd and explains why the animals are gathered together.

Snug Tales

Make up a tall tale about crowds or being crowded. Be sure to include some hilarious exaggerations. Add illustrations and share your tall tale with the rest of the class.

More Books

Arnold, Caroline. *Bat*. Morrow, 1996.

Fichter, George S. *Bees, Wasps, and Ants*. Western, 1993.

Fischer-Nagel, Andreas and Heiderose Fischer-Nagel. *An Ant Colony*. Carolrhoda, 1989.

Gallant, Roy A. *The Peopling of Planet Earth: Human Population Growth Through the Ages*. Macmillan, 1990.

Greer, Gery and Bob Ruddick. *This Island Isn't Big Enough for the Four of Us*. Crowell, 1987.

Lisker, Tom. *Terror in the Tropics: The Army Ants*. Raintree, 1977.

Park, Barbara. *My Mother Got Married and Other Disasters*. Random House, 1990.

On the Web

Animals
http://www.discovery.com/stories/nature/
    ants/ants.html
http://www.nwf.org/nwf/endangered/
    index.html

Population
http://www.facingthefuture.org/index4.htm
http://www.un.org
http://www.unicef.org

Across the Curriculum

Social Studies

Which parts of your state are the most crowded? Color-code an outline map of your state to show which places have the greatest and least population. Be sure to include a map key so readers can understand the information on your map.

Mathematics

If there were about six billion people on Earth in the year 2000, and we add about a billion more people every twelve years, how many people will be on Earth in 2012? In 2024? Make a graph that shows the approximate population on Earth during the 21st century.

Cramped Quarters

You Think You've Seen a Traffic Jam?

On February 16, 1980, a traffic jam in France stretched 109 miles. Traffic was at a standstill from Lyon to Paris.

Crowded Bug

At the University of Hawaii in 1998, 24 people crowded into a small-sized car sometimes referred to as a "bug"!

Crowded Car Rules

So how do people go about setting a world record for the number of people who can crowd into one car? Here are the rules they must follow:

- The car must be a regular automobile.
- They must be able to close the doors and windows after everyone is in the car.
- They have only 10 minutes to get everyone in the car.
- They must be able to start the engine after everyone is in the car.
- All the people must be at least 16 years old.

A Crowd of Hoops

On August 5, 1999, Lori Lynn Lomeli spun, at the same time, a "crowd" of 82 plastic hoops around her for three complete revolutions!